# Golf for Young Girls
## Mastering the Sports Psychology of Golf

# Phillip Chambers

# Contents

# Introduction

I n the bustling heart of Mexico City, where vibrant streets pulse with life and ancient traditions intermingle with modern ambitions, a young girl named Gaby Lopez dreamt of vast green landscapes, the quiet hush before a swing, and the thundering applause after a hole-in-one. This is her story, a tale that begins in the sun-soaked terrains of Mexico and takes us on a whirlwind journey to the most prestigious golf courses across the globe.

The streets of Mexico City were far from the serene green of golf courses. Yet, amidst the urban hustle, a passion for the game grew in Gaby. She wasn't born into opulence, and the path to golf stardom was rocky and steep, but young Gaby had something more potent than privilege: a fiery spirit, an innate talent, and a dream that was larger than life.

Her earliest memories of golf were with her father, a modest enthusiast of the game. Their weekends were sacred, dedicated to the sport. They couldn't afford the most upscale clubs or the latest equipment. But the duo had a bond, a shared love for the game that transcended materialistic needs. Under the vast Mexican sky, father and daughter would practice, laugh, and dream together.

As Gaby grew, so did her aspirations. But with dreams come challenges. In a country where golf wasn't the most celebrated sport and where female athletes often took the backseat, Gaby's ambition was met with skepticism. Many times, she was told to be realistic, to understand her 'limitations'. But every whisper of doubt only made her resolve stronger. She wasn't just playing for herself; she was playing for every girl who was told she couldn't.

Navigating the world of professional golf was like walking through a labyrinth for Gaby. The pressure was immense, and the competition was fierce. There were moments of self-doubt, days when the weight of her dreams seemed too heavy to bear. But every time she stumbled, she remembered the vast Mexican skies, the teachings of her father, and the fire of her dreams.

Like many young girls, maybe you've faced moments of doubt. Those times when you wonder if you're good enough or if you'll ever succeed. Gaby knows that feeling all too well. But she also knows that the fiercest battles are fought within. With every swing, with every tournament, Gaby trained her mind to be as strong as her swing. She believes that real victories happen within us, not just on the golf course.

Now, what if you could walk a mile in Gaby's sparkly golf shoes? What if you could learn her secrets to being mentally strong? This book isn't just about golf; it's about discovering your inner strength. Dive into the chapters, and you'll feel like you're unlocking a treasure chest, each section glittering with wisdom.

With every page, you'll journey deeper into Gaby's world. From the challenges she faced, the pressures she overcame, and the sheer willpower she harnessed to become the star she is today. You'll see that even in the vast world of golf, where male names often dominate the spotlight, Gaby shines brilliantly, inspiring young girls everywhere.

In this book, you'll go on a journey of self-discovery. You'll explore your own thoughts and feelings and find wisdom to help you improve your golf game. It's not just about learning the physical parts of golf, like swinging a club or making a perfect putt. It's about transforming your mind and becoming stronger and more patient. You'll learn eight important skills that will unlock different parts of your mental game, making you a better golfer and a more focused person.

These lessons come from studying the world's best golfers, like Tiger Woods, Phil Mickelson, and Gaby Lopez. They have faced tough times and public scrutiny, but they have always stayed mentally strong. The skills and strategies in this book are not just theories; they are practical steps that these great golfers have used to achieve their remarkable success.

Take Tiger Woods, for example. He's not just a golfer; he's a legend. Tiger's name is known all over the world, and his mental strength is as important as his golf skills. He has faced scandals and injuries, but he never gave up. He used his resilience to turn challenges into victories.

Or look at Phil Mickelson, another amazing golfer. He went through a six-year period without winning a major tournament, and people called him the best player to never win. But he didn't let that negativity bring him down. Instead, he used it as motivation and won the Masters in 2004. His story shows us how important a positive mindset can be.

Gaby Lopez, an LPGA professional, is another example of mental toughness. She knows that her biggest victories happen off the golf course, in her mind. She trains her mind to be strong, just as much as she trains her body. That's what has made her the great golfer she is today.

So, if you want to improve your golf game and become mentally tough like these golfing greats, this book is for you. You'll learn valuable lessons and strategies that will help you overcome challenges and become the best golfer you can be.

Each chapter of this amazing book is like a treasure map that will guide you to unlock the secrets of being mentally strong in golf, just like the incredible champions we admire. Are you ready for an adventure? Get ready to explore the power of focus, discover how failure can actually help you, learn how to handle pressure like a pro, and develop the awesome skill of adapting to any situation. These are the secret ingredients that transform a good golfer into a truly great one!

By the time you finish reading this book, you'll be a true expert in the mental game of golf. But it's not just about knowledge—it's about putting what you learn into action. This book gives you a special roadmap full of strategies you can actually use, cool stories you can relate to, and techniques that have been proven to work. It's not just a regular book; it's like a magical journey that will transform you into a better version of yourself, both on and off the golf course.

You might be wondering, "Why should I choose this book? There are so many others out there!" That's a great question! This book stands out because it takes a careful and complete approach to understanding the mental side of golf. The author did a lot of research, interviewed experts, and studied the most successful golfers to bring you the very best knowledge.

Are you ready to unlock the mysteries of the mind in golf? With every page you turn, you'll embark on an exciting adventure. You'll learn how your mind and body work together in golf, how being strong mentally can improve your swing, and how having a positive attitude can make your shots soar!

This book is your special key to unraveling the secrets of the mind in golf. Get ready for an incredible journey! Together, we'll explore the hidden side of golf that has been waiting to be discovered. We'll go from feeling confused and frustrated to feeling victorious and happy. We'll navigate through the twists and turns of the mental game of golf, from the challenging lows to the exhilarating highs. And remember, this journey is not just about becoming a better golfer—it's about becoming a better version of YOU. Let's get started!

# Chapter 1

# Mental Toughness in Golf

*In my opinion think of a calm song*

I magine a magical moment as the sun sets, painting the sky in breathtaking colors while a golf match reaches its final hole. The golfer stands there, surrounded by a hushed crowd and the click of cameras, with victory or defeat just a stroke away. This is where mental toughness becomes essential. Sweaty palms, a racing heart, and a whirlwind of thoughts may try to distract the golfer, but it's in these intense moments that they must stay calm, focused, and make the shot that can change everything. That's why Jack Nicklaus, an incredible golfer, once said, "Don't ever try to tell me golf is not 99.9 percent a mental game."

Jack Nicklaus knew what he was talking about. His amazing career wasn't just about physical skill or technique. It was his unshakable belief in himself, his ability to stay focused on what he could control, and his determination to always improve that led him to victory after victory. So, let's explore the fascinating world of mental toughness in golf and discover why Nicklaus believed it was such a critical part of the game.

Being mentally tough in golf means having a lot of different qualities like acceptance, patience, self-confidence, composure, focus, and control. Think of your mind as a beautiful garden, where each quality is a seed that needs nurturing and care to grow. We'll take a stroll through this garden, exploring each element and how they come together in the challenging world of golf.

You might wonder why golf is considered a mentally demanding sport. Well, in golf, you have plenty of time to think, but every shot counts. So, how do golfers find balance in this pressure-filled game? How do they handle frustration? And is there a right way to use positivity to improve performance? We'll answer these questions and more as we dive into the mental mechanics of golf.

But here's the thing: there's no secret formula for mastering the mental game. Just like a physical skill, mental toughness takes practice. It's about showing up every day, being open to learning, and constantly working on your mental approach. One bad day on the golf course doesn't define you, but how you bounce back and learn from it does.

Don't worry, though. Developing mental toughness in golf brings incredible benefits. It gives you access to the "zone," where you can stay calm under pressure, refocus after a bad shot, and ultimately enjoy the game even more. Timing is crucial, too. You need to be patient and alert, calm yet focused, and always keep the bigger picture in mind, no matter the challenges you face in the moment.

Throughout this book, we'll take you on a journey that goes beyond the physical aspects of golf. We'll explore the intangible world of mental toughness. Let's look at the story of Collin Morikawa, an up-and-coming star in golf, and his coach, Rick Sessinghaus. Their unique relationship is a fascinating study of how mental toughness can be nurtured and applied in the game, showing us the vital role our minds play in pursuing greatness.

Whether you're a young golfer dreaming of turning pro or a parent supporting your child's golfing passion, this journey will give you valuable insights into the mental battleground that defines the game of golf. So, come on! Let's tee off into the mysterious, challenging, and rewarding world of mental toughness in golf.

### It's All in Your Mind

Jack Nicklaus, a golfing legend, believes that the real power in golf comes from mental toughness. It's not just about swinging the club or making perfect shots; it's about having a strong mind. Nicklaus proved this time and again throughout his amazing career. As you face the challenges of golf or anything else in life, remember these important lessons from Nicklaus about mental toughness.

Nicklaus always stressed the importance of believing in yourself. He believed that mental strength meant focusing on your own abilities and not comparing yourself to others. It's not about what someone else can do; it's about what you can do. By tuning out distractions and staying focused on yourself, you can perform better on the golf course and in life.

Nicklaus also taught us that mental toughness isn't something you're born with; it's something you develop over time. His long and successful career in golf showed us the power of a strong mental game. He won his first major at a young age and his last when he was much older, proving that mental toughness can carry you through a lifetime of challenges.

Remember, mental toughness is not only valuable in golf but in all aspects of life. It can help you deal with school pressure, social situations, and even future career choices. Nicklaus's advice is clear: Believe in yourself, focus on getting better, and always play the long game.

Just like Jack Nicklaus used the power of his mind to become a golfing legend, you too have the ability to tap into your mental strength and reach your personal best. It's about discipline, resilience, and having confidence in yourself. So, the next time you step onto the golf course or face a challenge in life, channel your inner Jack Nicklaus and play your own game.

### **What It Takes to Be Mentally Tough in Golf**

Mental toughness is like a secret ingredient that can make a big difference in golf, and it's made up of several important qualities. These qualities include self-confidence, composure, focus, control, patience, and acceptance. Let's explore what these mean and how they can help you become mentally tough on the golf course.

Self-confidence is all about believing in yourself and your abilities. Even if you've had some bad shots, having confidence in your skills can make a huge impact on your performance. Take the example of Phil Mickelson, a professional golfer who won the British Open despite being behind at the start of the final day. His unwavering self-confidence helped him stay focused and win the championship.

Composure is a superpower in golf. It means staying calm and composed even when things don't go your way. Sometimes you'll hit a bad shot or have a tough round, but mentally tough golfers don't let those moments bring them down. Instead, they use those challenges as motivation to keep going and get better.

Focus is like a laser beam that helps you stay on track. Golf can be a long game, and it's easy to get distracted by the weather, the crowd, or other things happening around you. But mental toughness means staying focused on the task at hand. Imagine standing on the 18th tee, tied for the lead, with a noisy crowd cheering you on. A mentally tough golfer will block out those distractions and focus on their swing, the ball's path, and their game plan for that crucial shot.

Control means being in charge of your thoughts and actions on the golf course. It's about not letting frustration or doubt get in the way of your performance. For example, let's say you have to hit a challenging shot over a water hazard. A mentally tough golfer will stay in control, focusing on the shot instead of worrying about the possible consequences.

Patience is another important quality in golf. Sometimes things don't go as planned, and it takes time to improve. Being patient means staying calm even when you're not playing your best. It means sticking to your strategy and understanding that golf has its ups and downs, and things can turn around at any moment.

Acceptance is about understanding that mistakes happen and not dwelling on them. Even the best golfers make mistakes. Acceptance means learning from those mistakes without being too hard on yourself. For example, if you miss an easy putt, a mentally tough golfer will accept it, learn from it, and move on to the next hole with renewed determination.

In conclusion, mental toughness in golf is a combination of different qualities that work together to improve your performance. Just like physical training, you can develop and strengthen these mental skills over time. As a young golfer, cultivating these qualities can not only help you succeed in golf but also lead to a happier and more balanced life. And for parents supporting young golfers, understanding these qualities can help you encourage resilience, patience, and self-belief, which are valuable traits that go beyond the golf course.

### **Golf: The Ultimate Mental Challenge**

Imagine a sport that combines physical skill with an incredible mental test. A game that challenges your mind like no other. That's golf—a sport that demands more than just athleticism. Even the most gifted athletes from other sports struggle when they try to compete in golf professionally. Legends like Tony Romo, Michael Jordan, Ivan Lendl, and John Smoltz, despite their athletic prowess, found it tough to reach the highest level in golf.

So, what makes golf so different? Let's explore the unique attributes that set it apart from other sports:

***Lots of Time to Think:*** In most sports, players make quick decisions in the heat of the moment. But in golf, the ball isn't moving, giving players plenty of time to think before each shot. While this may seem like an advantage, it can lead to overthinking, which can disrupt a player's natural flow.

***Every Shot Counts:*** In other sports, one missed shot doesn't define a player's success. But in golf, every single shot matters. Each stroke directly affects the overall score, adding extra pressure and intensifying the mental challenge.

***Balancing Consistency with Frustration:*** Golf requires consistency, but it also comes with its fair share of frustration. Players strive to follow a consistent routine before each shot, paying attention to even the tiniest details. However, despite their efforts, shots may not always go as planned, leading to frustration.

***Levels of Arousal:*** The level of physical and mental readiness, known as arousal, can greatly impact a golf swing. If the level of arousal on the course differs from that during practice, it can affect a player's performance. Managing this fluctuation adds another layer of mental challenge to the game.

But that's not all! Golfers also need to tackle a multitude of variables. They must learn to use different clubs in various ways, adapt to different grass types, adjust to changing weather conditions, and play over extended periods of time. And let's not forget—golf is an individual sport. There are no teammates to rely on or share the burden with. Every decision and stroke rests solely on the player's shoulders.

These factors highlight the need to approach golf not only as a physical sport but also as a mental challenge. It's a game that requires players to navigate a maze of thoughts, emotions, pressures, and decisions while striving to perfect a skill that can feel counterintuitive and demanding. Understanding and mastering the mental aspect of golf is a crucial part of a player's journey to success. And just like any journey, it's best tackled one stroke at a time.

### **Unveiling the Truth About Mental Toughness**

There are many myths and misconceptions surrounding mental toughness that can confuse our understanding and hinder our growth. Let's break down these myths and explore the truth about mental toughness, tailored just for you, a teenager, and your parents.

*Myth 1: Mental Toughness is Admitting Weakness*

Some people believe that working on your mental game means admitting weakness. But that couldn't be further from the truth! Mental toughness is not about fixing flaws; it's about building skills, just like practicing a sport or an instrument. It's about enhancing your strengths and abilities to handle pressure and stress effectively.

*Myth 2: The Mental Bubble of Positivity*

Another common myth is that we can control every thought in our minds and create a bubble of positivity. But even the most successful people can't control every thought that pops up. What they have learned is to control their reactions to those thoughts. It's normal to have negative thoughts sometimes, but what matters is how you handle them. Acknowledge them, let them pass, and refocus on the task at hand.

*Myth 3: Emotional Control Means No Feelings*

Emotional control is often misunderstood as suppressing or denying feelings, especially the negative ones. But that's not true! Emotional control is about recognizing and understanding your emotions, and then managing how you react to them. Feeling nervous or anxious before a big game doesn't mean you're weak. It's a natural response. Emotional control comes in when you use strategies to prevent those nerves from affecting your performance negatively.

*Myth 4: Positive Thinking Guarantees Success*

Many think that simply thinking positive thoughts will lead to positive results. However, it's not as simple as repeating positive statements. Instead, try asking yourself constructive questions like, "What does success look like for me?" or "What steps can I take to perform at my best?" These questions focus on the process and help create a positive mindset without guaranteeing a specific outcome.

*Myth 5: Chasing Consistency*

Consistency is often seen as the key to success, but it's a myth! Life is full of variables that can change daily, affecting our performance. Instead of chasing consistency, it's more beneficial to cultivate adaptability. Being able to adjust and perform well under different circumstances is a valuable skill.

**The Truth about Mental Toughness**

Mental toughness isn't a secret formula that can be found overnight. It's a progressive journey of mindset and character. It's like building a muscle—it takes constant training and reinforcement over time. It's the repeated habits and mindset shifts that help you develop mental toughness and become strong and resilient.

By understanding these truths, you can work on building your mental toughness, not just for sports but also for life. It's about enhancing your strengths, managing your emotions, and developing a positive mindset. So, let go of the myths, embrace the truth, and embark on your journey to mental toughness!

### The Unbreakable Mindset of Phil Mickelson

Let's take a look at the inspiring story of Phil Mickelson, a golf legend who faced numerous setbacks on his path to success. Despite coming so close to victory, only to see it slip away time and again, Phil never gave up. It took him 12 long years to win his first major title, but he never lost hope. He kept grinding, improving his skills bit by bit, and eventually, he claimed multiple major titles. Phil's journey wasn't about finding some secret formula; it was about perseverance, patience, and having a strong mindset. And just like Phil, you can train your mind to be tough too. Here are some practical steps to follow:

*1. Winning in the Mind:* Becoming mentally tough is just as important as honing your physical skills. Look at Phil Mickelson's journey. It took him time, resilience, and mental toughness to finally achieve major success after facing setbacks.

*2. No "Secret" to Mental Toughness:* Building mental toughness isn't about uncovering a secret formula. It's about consistent practice and never giving up. Just like you train your body to become a better golfer, you must also train your mind to become stronger.

*3. The Past Doesn't Define You:* What happened yesterday doesn't matter. Whether you made a mistake, had a setback, or achieved a victory, the key to mental toughness is focusing on the present and bringing your best self to the current game.

*4. Master Your Breathing:* Controlling your breathing is crucial for mental toughness, especially in stressful moments. It helps reset your mind and body, allowing you to maintain focus and stay calm.

**5. *Maintain Positive Body Language:*** Keeping an upbeat physical demeanor, regardless of your performance, helps maintain a peaceful mindset. This mental toughness trait allows you to let go of the past and focus on the next move.

**6. *Monitor Your Self-Talk:*** Pay attention to what you're saying to yourself on the golf course. Replace negative self-talk with neutral or positive statements that keep your morale high and your focus sharp.

**7. *Use Neutral Thinking:*** Transition from negative to neutral thinking, as recommended by mental coach Trevor Moawad. This helps you avoid dwelling on bad shots and keeps your mind focused.

**8. *Celebrate Positive Shots:*** Remember and enjoy your successful shots. By keeping these positive memories at the forefront, you can easily overcome challenges.

**9. *Laugh Off Bad Shots:*** Don't let bad shots ruin your mood. Laugh them off and focus on the next one, keeping a cool head and steady pace.

**10. *Keep a Mental Game Scorecard:*** Instead of solely focusing on the score, evaluate your mental preparation and execution. Create a mental game scorecard that gives you points based on your mindset and performance, not just the result.

**11. *Stop Worrying About the Score:*** Sometimes, it's beneficial to set aside the scorecard and focus on enjoying the game. This relieves pressure and allows you to play more naturally.

**12. *Stop Comparing Yourself to Others:*** Comparisons often lead to discontent and pressure. Focus on your own progress and growth instead.

**13. *Post-Round Recap:*** Take a few minutes after each round to reflect on your game. Note your best shots and areas for improvement. This keeps your focus on continuous growth.

**14. *Read Golf Books:*** Reading can provide a fresh perspective, break old thought patterns, and upgrade your mindset.

**15. *Take a Break if Needed:*** If you feel overwhelmed, taking a break can be beneficial. It helps you reset, regain focus, and reignite your love for the game.

In conclusion, the "secret" to building mental toughness and winning in the mind isn't really a secret at all. It's a journey of consistent practice

### Unlocking the Zone: Mastering Your Mind

Imagine being in complete control of your game—confident, focused, and effortlessly executing every swing. That's what it means to be "in the zone" in golf. It's a mental state where everything clicks, and your performance soars. But here's the exciting part: entering the zone is a skill that anyone can develop. It's all about understanding how to maintain your focus, confidence, and control on the course.

When golfers possess mental toughness, they enjoy incredible advantages during competition. Let's explore some of these advantages:

**1. *Awareness of the Zone:*** Mentally tough golfers recognize the sensations that come with being in the zone and can intentionally immerse themselves in it.

**2. *High Self-Confidence:*** They believe in their abilities and have unwavering confidence in their capacity to perform exceptionally well.

**3. *Concentration:*** They fully immerse themselves in the present moment, giving their undivided attention to the task at hand.

**4. Focused Attention:** They can narrow their focus to one specific thought without getting distracted by outside influences.

**5. Effortless Execution:** Their swings flow effortlessly, and they let things happen naturally when it matters most.

**6. Emotional Control:** They remain calm and composed under pressure, displaying emotional stability even in intense situations.

**7. Clear Decision-Making:** They avoid overthinking, doubt, and indecision, making clear and decisive choices.

**8. Refocusing Ability:** They quickly bounce back and gather themselves after making a mistake or hitting a bad shot.

**9. Fun:** Regardless of their score, they find joy in playing the game and maintain a positive mindset.

Developing mental toughness isn't a one-time task—it's an ongoing commitment. It requires consistent practice, both during training sessions and competitive events. That's why top golf coaches now emphasize the importance of mental training.

In golf, mental fortitude extends beyond mere mindset—it becomes a part of your lifestyle. The discipline, confidence, and focus it cultivates allow you to fully embrace the present moment, execute your swings effortlessly, and calmly handle mounting pressure. A mentally tough golfer makes decisive decisions and quickly rebounds from setbacks.

Remember, every stroke you make in golf involves decision-making. From considering the distance and selecting the right club, to analyzing the wind direction and anticipating the ball's roll on the ground, mental toughness equips you to make confident and accurate choices.

Just as you practice your swing and develop strategies for your game, it's crucial to prioritize the development of your mental toughness. It's not about achieving a perfect swing—it's about building a resilient mindset that empowers you to elevate your game and enjoy it even more.

In the wise words of sport psychologist Bob Rotella, "Believe you can win, stay in the present, remain patient, and ignore advice from well-meaning friends." If you've put in the work to develop your mental toughness, have confidence in your abilities and stick to your game plan. Mental toughness is the secret sauce that can transform a good golfer into a great one. So, unlock the power of your mind, master your mental game, and unleash your full potential on the golf course.

### Perfecting Your Timing: The Secret to Success

In the captivating world of golf, timing is everything. It goes beyond the physical execution of your swing or the rhythm of your putts—it's about strategic decision-making and mental composure. The ability to seize the right moment and make choices that optimize your chances of success is what sets great golfers apart. Let's explore the art of timing and how it can transform your game.

### Mental Toughness: The Game Within the Game

One of the most crucial aspects of timing is mental toughness. It's about remaining calm and focused under pressure, embracing challenges as opportunities for growth. Whether you're facing a tough shot on the course or navigating a challenging day at school or work, developing mental toughness is key. Every hurdle is a chance to flex your mental muscles and come out stronger.

### Playing the Long Game

While timing is important in the present, it's equally vital to keep your eyes on the bigger picture. Don't lose sight of your long-term goals while navigating the immediate challenges. The secret is to play the long game, maintaining a clear vision of your end goal and persevering through the obstacles along the way.

**Leave the Past Behind**

In golf, dwelling on past mistakes can hinder your current game. Each shot deserves its own focus and attention, free from the weight of previous errors. Learn from your missteps but don't let them overshadow your current play. Approach each shot with fresh eyes and a renewed determination.

**Breathe and Build Routines**

Taking a moment to breathe deeply before each shot can work wonders for your composure. It helps steady your nerves and clear your mind, keeping you present in the moment. Additionally, building routines for each phase of your game turns them into habits, ensuring consistency even under pressure. Trust in your routines—they will guide you through the toughest challenges.

**Deliberate Practice: Quality Over Quantity**

Perfecting your game isn't just about practice; it's about deliberate practice. Focus on the quality of your practice sessions rather than their duration. Slow down and pay attention to every aspect of your game, from visualizing the swing to striking the ball. This principle of "going slow to go fast" will refine your skills and elevate your performance.

**Trust Your Process**

Having a shot routine and a process that you trust is invaluable. Whether it's a simple routine or a complex one, the key is to have unwavering faith in your method and apply it consistently—especially after the not-so-great shots. Commit to your process, just like the pros do, and watch your game soar.

## Mastering Mental Skills

In golf and in life, it's often mental toughness, not just technical expertise, that sets individuals apart. Recognizing this early on and working on developing key mental skills is crucial. It's about becoming not only a better golfer but also a more resilient and confident individual, equipped to navigate the challenges that life throws your way.

These lessons go beyond the green; they apply to every aspect of life. The principles of timing, mental toughness, long-term thinking, staying present, embracing the unpredictable, and playing to succeed can guide you to greatness, not just in golf but in all your endeavors. So, embrace the challenge, perfect your timing, and become a warrior both on the course and in the game of life.

### **Unleashing the Power Within: Collin Morikawa's Journey**

In the world of golf, physical skills usually take center stage, overshadowing the hidden gems that make champions truly extraordinary. But one story stands out—a tale of Collin Morikawa and his mentor, Rick Sessinghaus. They believed that mastering the mind was just as important as mastering the swing. Together, they embarked on a remarkable journey that would reveal the intangible power of the mental game.

Collin Morikawa was a golf prodigy, even at a tender age. When he was just eight years old, he joined forces with Rick Sessinghaus, an applied sports psychologist. Sessinghaus knew that there was an "intangible" factor that could take Morikawa's game to new heights—a factor that went beyond physical skills and technical perfection. It was the "mental game," an often-overlooked aspect of competitive sports.

With his unique perspective, Sessinghaus nurtured young Collin, focusing on the psychological side of the game. Morikawa recalls a pivotal lesson from his mentor: the power of word choice. "Rick has taught me so much mentally," Morikawa reflects. "The one thing that really sticks with me is how important word choice is. If we talk about 'nerves,' everyone has them. But how can you mentally transform that nervousness into excitement or focus?" This shift in mindset became crystal clear during the 70th hole of the PGA Championship, as Morikawa turned his nerves into unwavering focus, propelling him to a victory that left an indelible mark in golf history. Sessinghaus's teachings were validated, and their impact proved undeniable.

But Morikawa's education with Sessinghaus didn't solely take place on the driving range—it unfolded on the course itself. Sessinghaus believed in applied learning, making Morikawa practice under varying conditions, constantly challenging him and unleashing his creativity. "Being creative and hitting different shots with different lies taught me to think about the options available instead of making the same full swing every time, like on the range," Morikawa explains.

Sessinghaus also introduced Morikawa to the concept of the "flow state"—a state of complete absorption where performance reaches its peak and the mind operates on autopilot. While many view this state as elusive and fleeting, Sessinghaus taught Morikawa that it could be trained for, its triggers understood, and its magic replicated.

The culmination of Sessinghaus's teachings came during the final round of the PGA Championship. Sessinghaus, alongside Morikawa's agent, had a front-row seat, witnessing their protégé expertly navigate the course. "It was quite a journey," Sessinghaus reflects, not only referring to that triumphant day but also to the 15 years of hard work they had invested together.

In a world where success is often equated with physical prowess, Collin Morikawa and Rick Sessinghaus's journey serves as a captivating reminder. There is much more to winning than meets the eye. The intangible power of the mental game can often be the difference between a good player and a true champion. It's a lesson that every young athlete and their parents can hold close to their hearts—a reminder that the mind holds immeasurable potential waiting to be unleashed.

### Level Up: Strengthen Your Mental Game

Now that you understand the significance of mental toughness in golf, it's time to take action and boost your mental strength on the course. We'll break down these strategies into two categories: tips for coaches and tips for athletes. By putting these techniques into practice, you'll have a practical framework to apply the lessons we've learned so far.

**For Athletes:**

*1. Embrace a growth mindset:* Believe in your ability to continuously improve and see failures as stepping stones to success.

*2. Establish routines:* Create stable and consistent routines that help you stay focused and calm under pressure. Stick to these routines for a sense of stability.

*3. Practice mental skills:* Engage in regular mental exercises such as visualization and mindfulness meditation. These train your brain to stay focused and composed during the game.

*4. Challenge your beliefs:* Confront any misconceptions or negative beliefs you may have about mental toughness. Replace them with empowering and positive beliefs.

*5. Cultivate resilience:* Remember that resilience is key in golf. Embrace difficult shots and rounds as opportunities to learn and grow, rather than viewing them as failures.

Remember, mental toughness is not a destination but a journey. It's about consistent effort and improvement. Show up, put in the work, and strive to enhance both your mental and physical skills. Keep practicing, stay focused, and let your mental strength lead you to success on the golf course.

# Chapter 2

# Finding Your Focus

I magine stepping onto the golf course, the world around you fading into a blur. All your thoughts, movements, and breath align with one goal—to reach that distant focal point. In the words of Patrick Reed, a golfing powerhouse, it's not about competing against others, but about mastering the course itself. Golf is a delicate dance of precision, patience, and mental toughness, and this chapter will delve into Reed's wisdom on maintaining focus in golf and life. By adopting his strategies, you'll equip yourself to stay on course, both on the green and in the game of life.

Reed's approach revolves around understanding what to focus on and what to tune out, without forcing your mind into a specific place. One of his guiding principles is emphasizing the process over the outcome. Golf is a marathon, not a sprint. It's about every shot, every hole, and every round coming together to shape your overall performance.

But how do you determine where to direct your focus in this grand golfing marathon? And more importantly, how do you sustain that focus? Let's break it down.

In golf, visualizing the path of the ball and precisely envisioning where you want it to go is crucial. It's not just about physical accuracy; it's about honing your mental precision. By narrowing your attention to specific moments in time and focusing on what you can control, you can achieve better shots and elevate your performance. Cultivating and maintaining focus is a skill that can be developed over time. And it's not only about what happens on the course; what happens off the course also impacts your ability to stay focused. Balancing quiet moments for mental breaks with practicing on busier courses can help you build resilience against distractions.

To further enhance your focus in golf, it's essential to understand the three types of attention: internal, external, and neutral. Each type has its own impact on your game, and knowing how to utilize them effectively can give you an edge on the course. Taking inspiration from the legendary Tiger Woods, renowned for his mental fortitude and unwavering focus, you can learn to practice amidst distractions rather than in silence. This unique approach can help you maintain composure even in the toughest tournaments.

Just like golf, life demands focus, patience, and the ability to block out distractions. This chapter equips you with the tools to keep your eye on the ball, stay on course, and navigate through life's challenges—one stroke at a time. So get ready to fine-tune your focus and unleash your full potential on the golf course and beyond.

### A Formula for Focus: Mastering the Present

Have you ever wondered how some golfers stay so focused, even when the competition is intense? Take Patrick Reed, a champion golfer, for example. He has a winning mindset that revolves around one key idea: focus on the process, not the outcome. In this chapter, we'll explore Reed's formula for focus and learn how to apply it to our own golf games.

### Focus on the Process, Not the Outcome

Reed's secret to staying focused is simple but powerful. Instead of worrying about what others are doing or the final score, he directs his attention to the game itself. He focuses on his swings, strategies, and how he handles challenges. It's like having a laser beam of concentration on the things that matter most.

Sometimes our minds wander, and that's okay. But the key is to notice when it happens and gently guide our focus back to the present moment. We can't control everything that happens, but we can control how we respond. By observing our thoughts and then shifting our focus back to what we're doing right now, we can stay on track.

### Tuning into What Matters

Being aware of what's happening around us and within us is essential, but we shouldn't get caught up in it. Just like Reed, we can use the competition and pressure to fuel our focus, rather than letting it distract us. We acknowledge it, but we don't let it take over our minds. We stay in control.

### Focusing on the Long-term Perspective

Reed reminds us that golf is a marathon, not a sprint. It's not just about one game or one shot—it's about the whole journey. We need to see each moment as part of a bigger picture. Even if we miss a shot or have a bad game, it doesn't define us. What matters is how we learn and grow from it.

Remember, focusing on the process means giving our best effort in the present. We don't worry too much about the outcome or try to predict the future. We trust in our skills and training and accept whatever comes with grace and resilience.

By doing our best in each shot and each moment, we open ourselves up to surprising and rewarding success, just like Reed and other golfing heroes.

So, the next time you step onto the golf course, remember Reed's formula for focus. Stay in the present, focus on the process, and give it your all. Enjoy the journey, and let your dedication and resilience lead you to greatness.

### Knowing What to Focus On: Mastering the Mental Game

In the world of golf, focus is the secret ingredient that can take your game to the next level. It's like having a superpower that allows you to tune out distractions and perform at your best. But what exactly should you focus on, and how can you train your mind to stay on track? Let's find out!

### Ignoring External Distractions

In golf, there are many things happening around you that can grab your attention. Your playing partners might be goofing around, or the weather might be less than ideal. But here's the trick: you can choose to let these distractions slide off your back. It's all about fostering an internal locus of control, where you're in charge of your focus and not swayed by external factors.

### The Power of Pre-Shot Routine

Marvin Sangüesa, a pro golfer and coach, has a fantastic tip for staying focused: follow a pre-shot routine. This routine helps you get in the zone and tells your mind and body that it's time to focus on the task at hand. It could involve visualizing your shot, aligning your stance, and taking a few deep breaths to calm your nerves. By establishing a routine, you set yourself up for success.

### See It Before You Swing It

Visualization is like creating a movie in your mind. Before you hit the ball, imagine your perfect shot. Picture the trajectory, the landing spot, and the ball rolling smoothly towards the hole. This mental rehearsal boosts your confidence and primes your brain for success. So, take a moment to see yourself succeeding before taking your swing.

**Taming Your Thoughts**

Sometimes, our minds can wander to past mistakes or future worries. It's important to recognize these distractions and bring your focus back to the present moment. Julie Wells, an expert in the field, suggests using rituals or being aware of your self-talk. A quick ritual like grabbing a new golf ball or humming a tune can refocus your mind. And by keeping a positive and specific inner dialogue, you can prevent negative thoughts from affecting your game.

**The Power Lies Within**

Remember, focus is a mental game. It's not about being in a constant state of concentration but knowing how to bring your focus back when it wavers. The golf course is filled with external factors beyond your control, but your reaction to those factors is entirely up to you. Train your mind to let distractions float away and replace them with positive thoughts.

Now that you know what to focus on, go out there and unleash the power of your mind! Stay in the present moment, trust your abilities, and enjoy the game. With a strong mental game, you'll conquer the golf course and be ready to tackle any challenge that comes your way.

## Pinpoint Precision: Mastering Focus in Golf

In the world of golf, precision is key to success. It's not only about hitting the ball where you want it to go but also about training your mind to stay focused. Let's explore the importance of pinpoint precision and how you can develop it.

**Focusing on Your Focus**

Pinpoint precision starts with focusing on your focus. That means becoming aware of where your attention is directed and how it can wander. Golf courses are full of distractions like chirping birds and rustling leaves, but you can tune them out. By going inward and narrowing your focus, you can concentrate on what you can control—your attitude, preparation, and how you respond to challenges.

**Timing Your Focus**

Concentration in golf is like a secret weapon, but you don't need to be focused all the time. Golf is a marathon, and maintaining constant concentration can be tiring. Instead, focus on specific moments, like when you're preparing for a shot or analyzing the course. Between these times, give your mind a chance to rest and recharge.

**Triggering Your Focus**

To switch on your focus when it's time, create a trigger. It could be a gesture, a phrase, or even an object that tells your mind it's game time. When the task is done, let yourself relax and conserve your mental energy for the next round of focus.

**Remembering the Journey**

In golf, the journey is just as important as the destination. It's like a small version of life, teaching us about focus, precision, and control. Balancing the external world with your internal thoughts is the secret to success. So, when you step onto the green, keep your focus sharp, your control strong, and enjoy the game one mindful stroke at a time.

With practice, you can become a master of pinpoint precision. Train your mind to stay focused, and watch your golf game reach new heights. And remember, the skills you learn in golf can also help you in other areas of life. So, stay focused, stay determined, and enjoy the wonderful journey of golf!

## Staying Focused in Golf: Unleash Your Inner Golfer

Surrounded by beautiful landscapes and fierce competition, distractions are innevitable. As you embark on this mental journey, let's explore some strategies to enhance your focus and elevate your golf game.

**Dealing with Distractions**

Golf is a game of precision that requires laser-sharp focus. But distractions can sneak up on you, threatening to throw off your game. Fear not! Preparation is your secret weapon. Get to know the course inside out, study its twists and turns, and warm up with practice shots. This armor of preparation will shield you from distractions when you step onto the turf.

Sometimes, busy courses can overwhelm your senses. In those moments, seek out quieter spots or play during off-peak times. Finding the right balance between peaceful and lively courses can give you an edge.

**The Power of Mental Breaks**

Golf demands both physical and mental energy. It's essential to take regular mental breaks during your round. These breaks are like refreshing pit stops that recharge your mind and keep your focus sharp. Take a walk, stretch your muscles, hydrate, and practice deep breathing exercises to rejuvenate your mental prowess.

Remember, golf is a marathon, not a sprint. Divide your round into manageable chunks and use these breaks to rest and refuel. As the wise golfers say, "The real game begins at the back nine." So, stay refreshed and finish strong!

**Deliberate Practice Off the Course**

Improving your game doesn't stop when you leave the course. Off-course practice is just as valuable. But here's the secret: it's not about hitting a hundred aimless balls. Instead, focus on deliberate practice. Take your time, perfect your technique, and pay attention to every little detail of your game.

Patience is a virtue in golf. Rushing your shots can lead to mistakes. So, slow down, find your rhythm, and let the harmony of the game guide your performance.

## The Magic of Routines

Routines are like anchors that keep you grounded amidst the uncertainties of golf. Develop a pre-shot routine that sets the stage for your shot. But don't stop there. Create a post-shot routine too.

Golf is a roller-coaster ride of ups and downs. It's crucial to maintain your composure. After each shot, whether it's a hole-in-one or a miss, hit the mental reset button. Take a few deep breaths or repeat a positive affirmation to reset your focus and move forward.

## Setting Personal Boundaries

Golf is not only about your individual journey but also about respect and camaraderie with your playing partners. Set personal boundaries and communicate them to your fellow golfers. Ensure that everyone understands and respects your focus on the game. Treat each other with fairness and consideration. If a partner is struggling, offer support rather than taking advantage. Remember, golf is a game of integrity and etiquette.

## Keep Your Eye on the Bigger Picture

Golf is not just about hitting the ball. It's a journey filled with priceless moments of learning, self-improvement, and joy. Stay focused on the bigger picture—the love for the game. Embrace these tips, unlock your inner golfer, and let the magic of golf unfold before your eyes.

Now, step onto the green, stay focused, and embark on a thrilling adventure that will shape you as a golfer and a person. Enjoy the game, and may your focus guide you to golfing greatness!

## The Three Types of Focus in Golf: Unlocking Your Concentration Powers

In the exciting world of sports, focus is like a superpower that can help you achieve greatness. And in the game of golf, where every swing counts, focus becomes even more crucial. Today, we'll explore the three types of focus in golf: internal, external, and neutral. Let's dive in and see how each type can make you a better golfer.

### Internal Focus: Becoming a Swing Mechanic

Internal focus is all about understanding the mechanics of your golf swing. It's like learning a dance routine step by step. You pay close attention to how your body moves, such as how your wrists bend or how your shoulders rotate during the swing. This focus is useful when you're learning new techniques or fixing a swing flaw. But be careful not to overanalyze and make your swing feel awkward. Remember, you want your swing to flow naturally, like a graceful dance.

### External Focus: Hitting the Target

In external focus, you direct your attention to things outside your body. Instead of thinking about your swing, you focus on the impact your swing has on the ball, the ball's flight, or the target you want to hit. Imagine you're trying to avoid bunkers on the course. By focusing on keeping the ball away from the sand, your body naturally adjusts to make that happen. External focus helps you let go and allows your body to do what it knows best. It's like trusting your dance partner to lead you in the right direction.

### Neutral Focus: Find Your Zen

Neutral focus is a bit different. It's when you focus on something unrelated to golf, like your breathing or a catchy tune. It's like taking a mental vacation from the game. Let's say you're about to make a crucial putt under pressure. By humming your favorite song in your head, you can stay calm and focused, preventing those nerves from getting the best of you. Neutral focus is your secret weapon for staying cool when the pressure is on.

**Using Each Focus Type to Shine**

Now that you know about the three types of focus, it's time to use them to your advantage. When you're learning new skills or making swing adjustments, use internal focus to understand the mechanics. But during the game, switch to external focus to let your body do its thing naturally. And when you need to stay calm and focused under pressure, tap into the power of neutral focus. Each type of focus has its special place in your mental toolkit.

So, the next time you step onto the golf course, remember the power of focus. Pay attention to your body and swing mechanics when needed, but also direct your focus outward to hit the target. And when the game gets intense, find your Zen with a neutral focus. By mastering these three types of focus, you'll become a golfing superhero, ready to conquer any challenge that comes your way. Keep swinging, keep focusing, and let your golf game shine!

**Stories to Inspire: Embracing Distractions for Better Focus**

In the world of golf, there's a legendary player named Tiger Woods. He's known for his exceptional skills and ability to perform under pressure. But do you know one of his secrets to staying focused during games? It's a surprising idea that can teach us a valuable lesson.

Woods once compared playing golf to reading a book with the TV on. At first, it might sound strange. How can you concentrate with distractions around? But Woods isn't telling us to ignore the noise. Instead, he encourages us to embrace it and find focus amidst the chaos.

Imagine trying to read a book while the TV is on. You can still enjoy the story, even with the background noise. In the same way, Woods wants us to learn to focus even when there are distractions around us. It's about becoming comfortable with the noise and not letting it distract us from what we're trying to accomplish.

This approach might seem unusual, but it's actually quite wise. In real life, we often face distractions and pressures. We can't always find a perfectly quiet and peaceful environment. So instead of trying to eliminate the distractions, Woods teaches us to adapt and stay focused in any situation.

A golfer named Harold Varner III learned this lesson from Woods. He practiced his focus by reading with the television on, just like Woods suggested. By doing this, Varner learned to control his attention and concentrate even when there were distractions around him. It was a simple yet powerful strategy that we can all use.

So, the next time you find yourself in a distracting environment, remember Woods's advice. Don't get frustrated or try to block everything out. Instead, make peace with the distractions and learn to function within them. It's like turning a challenge into a strength, using the noise to enhance your concentration and performance.

This story from the golf course can inspire us in many aspects of life. Whether it's studying for a test, performing under pressure, or even just reading a book with the TV on, we can apply Woods's lesson. So embrace the distractions, stay focused, and let them become a part of your journey to success.

### Teeing Up: Steps to Sharpen Your Focus

We've learned how important focus is in golf, and now it's time to take action to improve our concentration on the course. Let's break it down into two parts: one for coaches and one for athletes. Get ready to tee up and enhance your focus skills!

**For the Athlete**

*1. Embrace the right perspective:* Remember that your main competition is the golf course, not just other players. Focus on your own game, your strategy, and your techniques.

*2. Master tuning in and out:* Train yourself to concentrate on the important aspects of your game while filtering out distractions. Practice visualization techniques to strengthen your concentration skills.

*3. Adopt a process-focused approach:* Don't just focus on the outcome. Pay attention to the steps you're taking to execute each shot. Stay in the moment and trust your process.

*4. Use different focus strategies:* Understand and practice using internal, external, and neutral focus. These techniques will help you perform at your best in various situations on the golf course.

*5. Take care of your off-course mental health:* Remember that your mental well-being outside of golf affects your focus on the course. Prioritize self-care and manage stress to maintain a clear and focused mind.

By following these steps, you'll be on your way to sharpening your focus skills and improving your golf game. So get out there, stay focused, and watch your performance soar!

# Chapter 3

# Controlling your Emotions

As the sun rose over the golf course, a Scottish voice filled the morning air. It was Robert MacIntyre, a rising star in the world of golf, sharing his wisdom with calm confidence: "Stay composed, deal with whatever happens, and keep swinging." MacIntyre's journey from a small coastal town in Scotland to the prestigious Augusta greens is a testament to the power of emotional strength in golf.

Emotions can be a game-changer on the golf course. Bobby Jones, a legendary golfer, once said that the real battle is fought in the five inches between your ears – your mind. It's the struggle within ourselves, the whirlwind of emotions that can make or break our game. When frustration or anxiety takes hold, it can lead to a string of bad shots and a negative mindset.

We've all seen players who let their emotions get the best of them – smashing clubs, throwing tantrums, or yelling in frustration. Instead of focusing on their game, they waste energy on emotional outbursts. It's like a battle between the emotional brain and the thinking brain, where emotions over-power rational thinking. That's where the skill of emotional mastery comes in.

But where do these emotions come from? Sometimes it's the pressure to be perfect, the fear of failure, or unrealistic expectations. It could also be stress from personal life or physical health issues. Understanding these sources is the first step to overcoming them and gaining mental clarity for peak performance.

Once we know where our emotions originate, the next step is managing them. Techniques like detachment, acceptance, and refocusing can help us avoid self-sabotage on the course. It's not about ignoring our feelings but acknowledging them, giving them their space, and then bringing our focus back to the game. Golf, like life, is a journey, and building emotional strength takes time. It's about having a growth mindset, recognizing our triggers, and finding ways to overcome them. Deep breathing exercises can also be helpful in calming our minds and strengthening our mental game.

Brooks Koepka, a professional golfer, has a great attitude: "It's just a game. I give it my best, and whatever happens, happens." He shows us the right approach to a tough day on the course.

Remember, you may not have direct control over your emotions, but you can control how you respond to them. That's emotional mastery – unlocking your true potential as a golfer. In this chapter, we'll delve deeper into these concepts, providing practical advice and strategies that you can use both on and off the course. We'll help you transform your approach to the game, making you not only a better golfer but also a more resilient person. Get ready to conquer your inner game and take your golfing skills to new heights!

**Personal Principles of Rob MacIntyre**

Robert MacIntyre, a professional golfer from Scotland, has a special approach that sets him apart. He believes that managing emotions is key to success on the golf course. Growing up in Scotland, where the weather and courses can be tough, MacIntyre learned the value of patience, perseverance, and staying calm.

Instead of letting emotions cloud his judgment, MacIntyre treats each shot as a separate event. He accepts the outcome, good or bad, and moves on with a clear mind. This helps him stay focused and prevents one bad shot from affecting the rest of his game. MacIntyre knows that getting too emotional can lead to poor decisions and hurt his performance. So, he focuses on the present moment, not dwelling on the past or worrying about the future.

MacIntyre believes that his principles can help golfers of all ages and skill levels. Whether you're a beginner or a seasoned player, managing your emotions is crucial. MacIntyre's own success on the golf course is proof that his approach works. He consistently ranks among the best golfers in the world, thanks to his discipline, skill, and emotional control. His message to all golfers is clear: you can't let your emotions control you. Instead, accept them, manage them, and concentrate on the shot in front of you.

In the challenging world of golf, MacIntyre's philosophy is a guide to emotional management. His achievements show the power of staying composed, accepting situations, and maintaining focus in the face of challenges. Whether you're playing golf or facing life's obstacles, remember to identify the issue, face it head-on, and keep going.

## How Emotions Weaken Players

Emotions can have a big impact on a golfer's game. When negative emotions like frustration, anger, or anxiety take over, they can mess up a player's swing and their focus. For example, frustration can make a golfer tense up, lose concentration, and rush their decisions, leading to even more mistakes. It's like getting on a "Bogey Train" where one bad shot leads to another, and the golfer's state of mind gets worse with each error.

Emotions can also affect a golfer's physical abilities. If a golfer feels anxious or angry, it can mess up their swing and make them inconsistent. Their body might react differently, affecting their tempo, focus, and decision-making on the course. Emotions can impact both the physical and mental aspects of the game.

Getting caught up in negative emotions wastes a golfer's energy. Instead of using that energy to focus on the next shot or enjoy the game, they spend it on negative thoughts and feelings. But there are ways to cope with these emotions. Deep breathing exercises, humor to lighten the mood, and mental exercises to stay focused on the present shot can help. It's important to remember that everyone, even professional golfers, experiences negative emotions on the course. Mistakes happen, but they don't have to ruin the game. Letting go of the idea that mistakes are catastrophic can help a golfer stay calm, focus on the next shot, and avoid getting stuck on the "bogey train."

Emotions can be a golfer's enemy or their friend. By recognizing and managing emotions effectively, players can make sure their emotions help, not hinder, their performance on the golf course.

### Identifying your Temperament

The world of golf is not just about skills and technique; it's also about emotions. Sometimes, players' temperaments can be quite colorful, especially when they get angry. Let's explore some common types of angry golfers and their reactions on the course.

First, there's the Smasher. When things don't go their way, they take out their frustration on the ground, using their club like a hammer. Each swing that falls short of their expectations shakes the course with their displeasure.

Then we have the Thrower. When their ball ends up in a bad spot, like among the trees, they can't help but launch their club through the air. Suddenly, the peaceful atmosphere turns into an accidental javelin field, with their clubs soaring higher than their golf balls.

Next is the Breaker. After a stray drive, they take their club and break it over their knee. They take the saying "break the game" a little too literally, as if punishing their club would fix their wayward shots.

Lastly, we encounter the Yeller. Every time they miss their target, whether it's ending up in a sand trap or going way off course, they let out a loud cry of frustration. Their shouts echo across the greens, creating an unintended soundtrack for the game.

However, these angry reactions do more harm than good. Uncontrolled negative emotions can tense up your body and mind, disrupting your focus and ruining your game. But the good news is that you can transform these emotions into opportunities for improvement.

See it as a challenge to master your emotional response. Focus on the next move and keep your mind in the present moment. Treat the next shot as a task that you can handle, and concentrate on putting yourself in the best position to play it. At the same time, find a sense of relaxation, allowing your mind to let go of negative thoughts and giving your body the freedom to swing.

Remember, anger doesn't have to be your downfall. Instead, use it as a stepping stone to becoming a better golfer.

**Inside Your Brain: Exploring Emotions and Thoughts**

In the game of golf, as well as in life, our emotions have a big impact on how we perform. Whether we feel happy, sad, excited, or frustrated, our emotions can affect our decisions, focus, and how well we play the game. To understand why this happens, we need to take a look inside our brain and learn about its different parts and how they work together. Let's use a fun metaphor to help us understand: the alligator and the computer.

Think of your brain as having two important parts: the alligator represents your emotional brain, and the computer symbolizes your thinking brain. Each part has its own job to do.

The alligator, or emotional brain, is responsible for our survival instincts and our emotional reactions. It's like a powerful creature that can make us feel happy, scared, or angry. On the other hand, the computer, or thinking brain, helps us make rational decisions and think logically. It's like a smart machine that helps us figure things out.

These two parts of the brain are constantly talking to each other and influencing each other. When something happens that makes us feel a certain way, the emotional brain reacts and sends signals to the thinking brain. The thinking brain then decides what action to take based on those signals. It's important for these two parts to work together smoothly so we can manage our emotions effectively.

Sometimes, though, the emotional brain can become too strong and overpower the thinking brain. This is what we call emotional hijacking. When the emotional brain senses a threat, like a bad shot in golf, it can take control and make us feel stressed or afraid. This can make it harder for the thinking brain to make logical decisions and think clearly.

Our thoughts, emotions, and actions are all connected in a cycle. Our thoughts can influence how we feel, and our emotions can affect how we act. And the actions we take can also shape our thoughts and emotions.

When we think positively and have optimistic thoughts, we tend to feel good. On the other hand, negative thoughts can lead to negative emotions. And our emotions can impact how we behave. For example, if we feel frustrated after a bad shot, we might act impulsively or lose control.

But here's the interesting part: our actions can also affect our thoughts. When we do something well, like hitting a great shot in golf, it can boost our confidence and make us think positively about our abilities.

Understanding how our thinking brain and emotional brain work together is important. It helps us develop strategies to manage our emotions effectively, improve our performance in golf, and feel better overall.

So, remember, inside your brain, the alligator and the computer are always working together. By learning to understand and control your emotions, you can become a better golfer and have more control over your thoughts and actions. Keep practicing and learning, and you'll see how your brain can help you play the game with focus and joy!

### **Where do Emotions Come From?**

Emotions are a fascinating part of being human. They come from a combination of different factors that shape how we feel. When it comes to golf, these factors become even more important because the sport requires both physical skill and mental strength.

In life, we experience a range of emotions. Sometimes we feel happy, excited, or proud, while other times we may feel sad, disappointed, or frustrated. These emotions can have a big impact on how we play golf. For example, when we make a great shot, we might feel joy and satisfaction. But if we miss an important putt, we might feel disappointment or frustration.

Our emotions in golf are connected to many different things. Our personal expectations play a big role. We might have high hopes for a tournament or a game, and that can put pressure on us to perform well. This pressure can create feelings of anticipation, excitement, or anxiety. If things don't go as planned, we might feel disappointed or stressed.

Another factor that affects our emotions in golf is the desire for perfection. Many golfers want to make every swing and every putt perfectly. They strive for flawless performance. While this can lead to feelings of accomplishment and satisfaction when things go well, it can also bring frustration and self-doubt when we make mistakes. It's important to remember that perfection is not always possible, and it's okay to make mistakes and learn from them.

Our emotions are influenced by our physical well-being, our experiences, and the environment we're in. The key is to understand that emotions are a natural part of the game and to find ways to manage them effectively. By recognizing our emotions and finding strategies to stay focused and positive, we can improve our performance and enjoy the game even more.

So, the next time you step onto the golf course, remember that emotions are a normal part of the game. Embrace the joy of success and learn from the challenges. Golf is not just about swinging a club; it's also about understanding and managing your emotions. And by doing that, you'll become an even better golfer and have more fun along the way!

### **Physical Health: A Foundation for Success**

The condition of your body has a big impact on how you feel emotionally, especially in sports like golf. When you're in pain or feeling tired, it can be frustrating and affect your mood. It can also impact your performance on the golf course, making it harder to enjoy the game. On the other hand, when you take care of your physical health by eating well and staying active, it can improve your mood, energy levels, and overall emotional well-being.

**Fear: Facing the Challenge**

Fear is a powerful emotion, and it's something that many golfers experience. It can come in different forms, like fear of not performing well, fear of not meeting expectations, or fear of getting hurt. Golfers may also fear choking under pressure, especially in important games or tournaments. This fear can increase stress levels, which can negatively affect your physical performance and mental focus. Fear is a natural response to potential threats, but in golf, it can hold you back and make it harder to play your best.

**Overcoming the Fear of Choking**

One common fear in golf is the fear of choking, which is when you underperform because of pressure or stress. This fear can come from high-pressure situations, difficult courses, or critical shots. It can become a self-fulfilling prophecy, meaning the more you fear it, the more likely it is to happen.

This fear often ties back to perfectionism and the expectations you have for yourself. When you strive for perfection and set high expectations, you put a lot of pressure on yourself, making it more likely that fear and choking will occur. Instead, try to have a more balanced perspective. Accept that mistakes happen and that they're part of the learning and growth process. This can help reduce the intensity of fear and the likelihood of choking.

Dealing with fear requires a combination of mental and emotional strategies. One approach is to shift your focus from the outcome to the process. Instead of worrying about the result or trying to be perfect, focus on the things you can control, like your swing, breathing, and mental routine. Practicing mindfulness and relaxation techniques can also be helpful.

They can keep you present in the moment, reduce anxiety, and prevent fear from undermining your performance.

Remember that your mindset off the course can affect how you feel on the course. If you're dealing with a lot of stress in other areas of your life, it can carry over to your golf game and increase your fear. That's why it's important to take care of your overall well-being. Maintain a healthy lifestyle, nurture positive relationships, engage in activities that reduce stress, and seek help when you need it. Taking care of your mental health is just as important as honing your physical skills in golf.

By prioritizing your physical health and cultivating a positive mindset, you can build emotional resilience, reduce fear, and enhance your performance and enjoyment of the game. Remember, golf is not just a physical game but also a mental one. Taking care of both aspects will help you excel on the course and in life.

### The Art of Controlling Emotions in Golf

Controlling your emotions is an essential skill in golf, and it can greatly impact your performance on the course. Emotions, thoughts, and behaviors are interconnected, and understanding this connection is the first step in gaining control over your emotions.

### Mindfulness: The Key to Emotional Control

Mindfulness is a powerful tool that helps you become aware of your thoughts, feelings, and emotions without being overwhelmed by them. It allows you to redirect your focus and accept your experiences, cultivating emotional agility.

### Navigating the Emotional Landscape

When you notice the onset of an emotion, such as anxiety or anger, acknowledge it by saying to yourself, "I feel anxious" or "I feel angry." This act of acceptance and self-compassion is the first step in gaining control over your emotions. Remember that emotions are temporary and will pass.

### Identifying the Source

Try to identify the source of your emotions. Often, they are triggered by external factors or past experiences rather than your current performance. Understanding the source can help neutralize the emotional impact and prevent it from affecting your perception and game.

### A Step-by-Step Approach to Controlling Emotions

*1. Acknowledge:* Take a moment to identify your thoughts and feelings without judgment.

*2. Accept:* Recognize that your thoughts and feelings are valid and okay.

*3. Identify:* Reflect on why you might be feeling a certain way.

*4. Reset:* Bring yourself back to the present moment by focusing on your breathing, smiling, or using positive affirmations.

### Realign and Refocus

After acknowledging and accepting your emotions, it's time to realign and refocus. Shift your attention to the next shot, focus on the process rather than the outcome, and adjust your expectations accordingly.

### Remember, Golf is About the Journey

Golf is not just about making perfect shots or winning matches. It's about enjoying the journey, the experience, and the joy of playing. Keep in mind that making mistakes is a natural part of the game. Set reasonable goals, be honest about your skills, and embrace the learning process.

When emotions threaten to overwhelm you, take a deep breath, smile, and swing. Remember that you're fortunate to be playing a beautiful game on the green. By controlling your emotions and staying focused, you'll enhance your game and enjoy the experience to the fullest.

### Building Emotional Strength and Control

Emotional strength and control are essential for golfers of all levels, from beginners to professionals. Just like physical skills, emotional management must be practiced and strengthened to enhance your game. Let's explore how you can build emotional strength, maintain stability, and foster a growth mindset to excel in golf.

**Understanding the Importance of Emotional Control**

Think of your favorite professional golfer. Broadcasters often mention the significance of emotional control for their success. The same applies to us. If we let our emotions take over, our game will suffer. Negative emotions can hinder focus and impact performance. This was a challenge I faced in my professional golf career.

**Golf: An Emotional Game**

Golf is not just about physical skills—it's also an emotional game. Understanding and managing your emotions can give you a significant advantage on the course. Three factors make emotional management in golf particularly challenging: you're alone without teammates to rely on, there's plenty of time between shots for overthinking, and stress hormones like adrenaline and cortisol don't always benefit golfers.

**Building Your Emotional Muscles**

To manage emotions and improve your game, start building your emotional muscles. Just like physical training, it takes practice and persistence. But once developed, these "muscles" will enhance your talent and efforts. Here's how:

*1. Self-Awareness and Tracking Your Triggers:* Understand your strengths, limitations, and triggers. Identify areas where you excel and challenges you face. Be aware of specific situations that trigger negative reactions. Awareness helps you make better decisions on the course.

*2. 90-Second Rule:* When emotions rise, apply the 90-second rule. Research shows that an emotional reaction lasts around 90 seconds. When you sense an emotion intensifying, take a deep breath and allow it about 90 seconds to naturally subside. This helps you manage and alleviate emotions, preventing them from affecting your performance.

**3. Staying Present:** Avoid distractions and emotional turmoil by focusing on the present moment. While goals are in the future, achieving them requires fully engaging in and embracing the present.

**4. Breathwork:** Deep, intentional breathing is a valuable tool for calming nerves and strengthening your mental game. It stabilizes emotions, improves focus, and enhances overall performance.

Building emotional strength takes time and practice, but it unlocks your full potential and elevates your golf game. Remember, success in golf isn't solely about physical skill—it also requires emotional strength and control. Start building your emotional muscles today and watch your game soar to new heights.

### Stories to Inspire: When Bad Days Happen—The Tale of Brooks Koepka

Golf is like a reflection of life itself—unpredictable, challenging, and sometimes frustrating, but also thrilling. It's a sport that requires not only physical skill but also mental strength. Let's explore the inspiring story of Brooks Koepka and how he handles unexpected defeat with grace.

Brooks Koepka is a celebrated golfer known for his physical abilities, unyielding confidence, and mental toughness. However, what truly sets him apart is his remarkable ability to navigate through tough times. One instance that stands out is his experience at the Masters in Augusta. It was a day that tested his resilience. Brooks had been playing exceptionally well, sinking putts and hitting accurate shots. His victory at the LIV Golf event prior to Augusta boosted his confidence, and he entered the Masters with a sense of momentum. Going into the final round, he held a two-shot lead over Jon Rahm from Spain.

But golf, like life, can be unpredictable. Despite his impressive performance leading up to the final round, Brooks fell short of winning the green jacket. His usually impeccable game seemed slightly off, resulting in a final round score of 3 over par, 75. Meanwhile, Jon Rahm seized the opportunity and won the tournament, turning a setback into an eagle on the very next hole.

Defeat can be disappointing, especially when victory seemed within reach. However, Brooks's mental toughness shone through. During his post-round press conference, he gracefully acknowledged his effort, saying, "I tried my hardest, gave it my all." This display of resilience and humility was truly inspiring.

Brooks's approach to bad days is one of acceptance and optimism. He understands that after good rounds, there can be bad ones. A single unfortunate swing or an unexpected turn can change the game's outcome dramatically. Instead of dwelling on what went wrong, he focuses on giving his best effort every time. His philosophy centers around resilience. No matter how tough the round or high the stakes, he remains committed to giving his all, unafraid of failure in his pursuit of success. This mindset is something every aspiring golfer, and every teenager, should strive to emulate. Brooks Koepka teaches us that setbacks should never stop us from giving our best.

In the bigger picture, your score is just a number. What truly matters is the process, the lessons learned, and the strength to bounce back when things get tough. Brooks Koepka's story vividly illustrates that bad days are part of life. How we handle those bad days and respond to failure defines who we are. His inspiring journey demonstrates the power of resilience and mental strength. When bad days happen—as they inevitably will—remember his story. Use it as a reminder to stay on your path, give your best, and most importantly, be gracious in both victory and defeat.

**Teeing Up: Actionable Steps to Master Your Emotions For Athletes:**

*1. Understand Your Emotions:* Learn about how emotions can impact your performance. Recognize how negative emotions can hinder your play and identify the common emotional responses that affect your game.

*2. Track Your Emotional Triggers:* Keep a record of situations when you become emotionally overwhelmed during a game. By understanding what triggers your emotions, you can develop strategies to better manage these situations.

*3. Practice Emotional Control Techniques:* Utilize techniques like the 90-second rule to allow your emotions to pass, practice deep breathing exercises to calm yourself, and learn to accept your feelings without judgment.

*4. Adopt a Growth Mindset:* Embrace a growth mindset and view challenges as opportunities for improvement. Avoid dwelling on mistakes and redirect your focus towards extracting valuable lessons from them.

*5. Work on Your Emotional Strength:* Develop strategies to strengthen your emotional control. This could include maintaining a mental scorecard to stay focused on the process rather than the outcome, adjusting your expectations, or seeking support from a mental performance coach if needed.

Remember, mastering your emotions is a skill that requires consistent practice and effort, just like any other aspect of golf. As you begin implementing these steps, you will gradually notice improvements in your ability to manage your emotions on the golf course, leading to better overall performance. Stay committed to the process, and enjoy the journey of emotional growth and enhanced golfing performance.

# Chapter 4

# Mastering Discipline

"There is beauty in tomorrow," Tiger Woods once said, emphasizing the value of continuous improvement. But what does it really mean to be better tomorrow? Is it simply hoping for a brighter future, or is it something more profound—a commitment to discipline, focus, and unwavering dedication to mastering one's skills? In this chapter, we will delve into Woods' philosophy, unveiling the intricate dance between time management, discipline, and mental toughness.

Tiger Woods, renowned for his mental strength as well as his physical prowess, wielded discipline like a finely tuned instrument. With unwavering commitment and resilience, he achieved victories in the face of fierce competition and personal challenges. His belief in being better tomorrow wasn't just about improving his swing or putting accuracy; it was a testament to the power of discipline and the relentless pursuit of mental toughness.

Imagine a golfer on a practice range, the sun setting and casting long shadows. With a bag of balls at their side, they carefully select one, position it, step back, swing, and observe as it soars through the air. This routine is more than just practice—it's a display of discipline. It signifies an understanding that excellence, much like a refined swing, requires disciplined practice. However, the path of discipline is not a popular one, especially for younger golfers.

Think of being in a casino. Most golfers, especially young ones, approach the game like gamblers, hoping for one lucky swing or one exceptional game. But discipline demands that we become the casino instead—consistent, strategic, understanding that small decisions made consistently lead to significant achievements. This shift in perspective requires embracing the mundane and repetitive aspects of practice in pursuit of greatness.

But how does one cultivate discipline? Envision yourself preparing for a shot. You assume your stance, focus solely on the ball, and in that moment, everything else fades away. The crowd becomes a distant hum, and your opponent becomes a mere blur in your peripheral vision. This is discipline—a combination of focus and consistency—a mental state that remains steadfast, directing your mind and body toward your goal.

With each repetition, each disciplined thought and action, you are ingraining routines and replacing old habits with better ones. A routine goes beyond a series of actions; it represents a purposeful sequence—a meticulously choreographed set of precise movements that, when consistently executed, becomes a defining characteristic of your playing style.

There are stories of golfers whose disciplined approach has led them to remarkable success. Consider the journey of Jon Rahm, who through discipline, learned to combine his raw talent with emotional self-control. His story exemplifies the transformative power of discipline in channeling one's emotions and skills to reach the pinnacle of the game.

In the following sections, we will explore these concepts further, delving into the intricacies of discipline and its connection to mental toughness. We will examine how discipline shapes the journey from the practice range to the hallowed greens of the Masters. This exploration represents our quest for the beauty of tomorrow—a disciplined journey toward becoming the best version of yourself.

### What's the Deal with Discipline?

Discipline may sound daunting, but it's actually a crucial element that connects success and progress in various areas of life, including golf. At its core, discipline is the practice of training oneself to follow a specific code of behavior or conduct. It involves consistency, dedication, and a commitment to a particular routine or set of tasks. In golf, discipline translates into a routine of consistent actions, practices, or behaviors. This consistency is essential for executing successful shots, precise putts, and well-timed swings. Essentially, discipline is the ability to repeatedly perform the same tasks in the same order, effectively and reliably.

### The Power of Routine

Creating routines is a significant aspect of discipline. Routines become familiar, comfortable, and something we can trust to yield consistent results. For example, think about your morning routine when you wake up—it's likely a series of habitual actions that you follow automatically. The same principle applies to golf. By establishing a disciplined routine in the game, such as a pre-shot routine, we reduce the need for excessive thinking, increase trust in our abilities, and execute actions with greater ease and confidence.

Developing discipline in your golf game requires a dedicated approach to practice, a willingness to learn, and the ability to eliminate distractions. The pre-shot routine is a prime example of discipline in golf. It's a consistent process that mentally and physically prepares you for each shot. When performed consistently, it creates a sense of predictability and control, elevating your overall performance.

A disciplined pre-shot routine may involve assessing the environment, selecting the appropriate club, visualizing the shot, aligning yourself, taking practice swings, and finally, executing the shot. Repeating this routine consistently builds familiarity and confidence, increasing the likelihood of success. Discipline isn't confined to golf—it's a valuable life skill applicable to various aspects of our lives. Whether it's studying for tests or working towards fitness goals, discipline, which involves repeating a specific set of tasks in a specific order and making them a routine, greatly enhances the chances of achieving desired outcomes.

Discipline is not about punishment or restriction; it's about fostering consistency, reliability, and, ultimately, success. By embracing discipline, both on and off the golf course, we pave the way for improvement, proficiency, and accomplishment. Remember, it's not just about hitting the perfect shot in the grand scheme of things; it's about embracing the journey that leads to it—a journey shaped by the well-placed strokes of discipline.

### The Significance of Discipline in Golf

Discipline in golf encompasses much more than simply showing up for practice sessions at the driving range. It plays a vital role in developing mental toughness, a crucial attribute that extends beyond sports and permeates all areas of life. In golf, as in life, mental toughness distinguishes mere participants from true achievers. For young golfers and their parents, recognizing the importance of discipline is the first step on a transformative journey that can shape both their game and their lives.

Golf, as a sport, possesses a unique ability to instill discipline due to its solitary nature. It is the player, the club, and the ball. There are no teammates to rely on or coaches to guide during play. In these quiet moments, players learn to manage their thoughts and emotions, leading to heightened mental toughness. Discipline in golf is not solely about physical consistency; it is about the mental fortitude required to persevere, even in the face of daunting odds.

For young golfers, discipline serves as the catalyst for transcending their current skill level. A golfer may have a flawless swing, but without the discipline to maintain focus, adapt to changing conditions, and continuously strive for improvement, that swing holds little value. Discipline fuels the drive to identify and work on weaknesses. It compels players to dedicate time to refining their short game when they might prefer driving balls or to practice challenging shots instead of cruising through easier rounds.

### Discipline Goes Beyond Consistency

Imagine a scenario where a golfer makes a poor shot. An undisciplined player might react in frustration, allowing disappointment to influence subsequent shots, resulting in a downward spiral of poor performance. In contrast, a disciplined player sees this as an opportunity for learning and growth. They take a moment to analyze what went wrong and how they can improve. This approach, built on discipline, transforms an error into a valuable learning experience, cultivating mental resilience over time.

Golf also teaches discipline through the process of setting and achieving goals. These goals may involve mastering a particular skill or attaining a specific score in a tournament. When a player sets a goal, they make a personal commitment to themselves. The discipline to uphold this commitment and persevere in the face of challenges is a vital aspect of personal growth and development. In this sense, the golf course becomes a classroom for character development, imparting life lessons that extend beyond the boundaries of the sport.

Discipline is also crucial in maintaining focus and resisting distractions. During a tournament, golfers must remain concentrated on their own game, regardless of how their competitors are performing. The discipline required to keep their minds from wandering or succumbing to anxiety showcases their mental control, turning each tournament into not just a competition with other players but also a personal test of their discipline and mental toughness.

Discipline in golf extends beyond the physicality of practice; it forms the foundation of mental toughness and personal growth. It transforms the sport into a lifelong journey of learning and development. For young golfers and their parents, embracing this aspect of the game can be the most rewarding part of their golfing journey.

Discipline can be tough, whether in golf or in other parts of life. It's about knowing what to do and actually doing it, even when things get difficult. Let's imagine it like steering a boat in a stormy sea. The waves are crashing, and the wind is strong, but you have a clear direction in mind. Staying on course can be really hard. It takes focus, making adjustments, and not giving up, even when things get tough.

In golf, young players are often like excited sailors, eager to explore the sea of the golf course. They have talent and enthusiasm, but they might not have a clear plan. It's like going to a casino and relying on luck to win against the odds. Golf is not about luck; it's about strategy and making smart decisions. It's like a sailor who knows how to read maps and navigate the waters. In golf, it's about making small choices, like which club to use or when to play it safe or take a risk. These choices might seem small, but they add up and lead to big achievements, just like a captain making small adjustments to steer their ship to the right destination.

Golf is not about taking big risks or relying on one lucky shot. It's about making consistent, thoughtful decisions. It's like a casino that makes small profits over time instead of depending on one big win. If young golfers learn this approach early on, they will play like smart strategists, always working towards their goals. Winning in golf comes from a calm, calculated strategy, not from flashy tricks or luck.

Discipline in golf means being consistent, staying strong even when things are tough, and thinking strategically. It's like being the captain of your own ship, navigating through challenges and making smart choices. It's about looking beyond the immediate shot and thinking about the long-term game. It's about being willing to take calculated risks and sticking to your plan, even when it feels like the odds are against you. And most importantly, it's about understanding that big goals are achieved through small, consistent, strategic decisions over time.

Discipline can be tougher for young athletes, including young golfers. It's because they often hear about instant success and big victories, which can make it hard to appreciate the power of small actions and consistent behavior in reaching their goals. It's like trying to explain to a young, vibrant tree that its real strength lies in the slow, steady growth of its roots beneath the surface, not just in its beautiful blossoms or sweet fruits. Similarly, young golfers need to understand that greatness comes from doing the same things repeatedly, making small improvements, and staying consistent in their efforts.

It's natural for young golfers to be drawn to the spectacular shots and winning trophies. But true mastery in golf, and in life, comes from paying attention to the small decisions made on the golf course. Each choice, from selecting the right club to adjusting their stance and swing, is like a building block in a strong foundation. These small decisions may seem boring or unimportant on their own, but when combined over time, they create a solid base for success.

While winning is important and boosts confidence, it's important to understand that success is not just about one big victory. It's the result of countless hours spent on perfecting the basics, making the right choices, and sticking to a good strategy. In golf, as in life, there are wins and losses. That's where mental toughness comes in. Mental toughness is like a lighthouse that helps young golfers navigate through tough times, setbacks, and disappointments. It reminds them that setbacks are part of the journey and don't define their potential. With mental toughness, they can stick to their plans, keep practicing, and trust in the process, even when immediate success doesn't come.

Teaching discipline to young golfers is like giving them the tools they need to sail through the challenges of the game. It's about helping them understand that greatness is built on small, consistent actions and decisions, supported by mental resilience and a strong commitment to the game. Instead of being like a gambler who lives for the moment, they should strive to be like a steady, resilient casino, playing for the long-term rewards.

The key to developing discipline in golf lies in both understanding your thoughts and emotions and following a strategic guide. It's not just about physical skills; it's about having the right mindset and approach to the game.

To develop mental discipline, start by being mindful of your thoughts and emotions. Just as you study the course before playing, examine the landscape of your mind. Practice being present and aware without judgment. This helps you direct your focus effectively and keeps your mind steady, like framing a picture.

Here arc some strategies to build mental discipline in golf:

*1. Control Fear:* Don't let past experiences dictate your game. Visualize success and feel the emotions of triumph to dispel any fear.

*2. Uphold Integrity:* Follow the rules of golf and maintain a code of conduct. This promotes self-esteem and minimizes distractions. Being honest about your performance creates a respectful and focused mindset.

*3. Employ Course Management:* When you're not playing your best, take a conservative approach. Strategically position your shots to increase your chances of a lower score.

*4. Maintain Present-Moment Focus:* Leave your ego at home and stay focused on the present. Replace self-doubt with positive affirmations like "I can..." or "I am..."

*5. Play the Odds:* Choose shots that you're confident in to avoid difficult situations. Assess the risks and make decisions based on your abilities.

*6. Be Decisive:* After analyzing all the factors that influence your shot choice, trust your decision. Doubt can only undermine your performance.

By practicing these strategies, you can develop the mental discipline needed to improve your golf game. Remember, discipline is not just about physical skill; it's about having the right mindset and approach to the game.

### Discipline like a Tiger

Tiger Woods, a legendary golfer, shows us the importance of disciplined thinking. Despite facing challenges, he won the

2019 Masters because he stayed focused and disciplined. Like Woods, we can train our minds to stay focused and manage distractions. Talking to ourselves about our strategy and goals for each shot can help us stay disciplined and perform our best.

Developing discipline in golf means directing our focus, controlling our emotions, and staying mindful. By mastering these skills, we can improve our performance and enjoy the game even more. These mental strategies in golf can also be applied in other areas of life where focus, discipline, and resilience are important.

Creating routines is an important part of discipline. When we do something consistently, it becomes a habit. Discipline helps us stick to our routines, even when it gets tough. Routines help us replace bad habits with better ones, making us stronger and more successful.

In golf, we can have routines for different parts of the game. We have a warm-up routine to prepare our bodies and minds. We have a routine before each shot where we plan and execute our strategy. After the shot, we analyze and learn from it to plan our next move.

By developing discipline and routines, we can improve our golf game and achieve our goals. Remember, discipline is like an internal compass that guides us through distractions. It helps us stay focused, consistent, and resilient. So, let's embrace discipline and watch our game reach new heights!

Improving your game requires developing routines that boost your performance. Here are three important steps to follow:

*1. Analyze your game:* Take a closer look at how you play. Figure out your strengths and weaknesses. Learning from each game helps you grow and get better.

**2. Identify areas to improve:** Be honest with yourself and find areas that need work. These become your focus for practice and improvement.

**3. Create a practice plan:** Plan your practice sessions smartly. Set aside specific time to work on each weakness and enhance your strengths.

Remember, it's not just about technical skills. Other things like being physically fit, mentally tough, and thinking strategically also impact your game. Make sure your routine covers all these aspects to maximize your improvement.

## Stories to Inspire: John Rahm—Keeping Calm With Discipline

Once in a while, we come across an amazing story of transformation and triumph in sports. The journey of Jon Rahm, who won the U.S. Open Golf Championship, is one such inspiring tale. Rahm used to struggle with his temper and impatience on the golf course, hindering his performance despite his talent. But everything changed when he became a father to his son, Kepa.

Being a dad made Rahm realize the importance of being a role model. He decided to leave behind his temper tantrums and embrace emotional self-control and discipline. This shift had a profound impact on his game.

During the U.S. Open, Rahm displayed remarkable composure and made incredible birdie putts. These moments will forever be remembered in golf history. His secret? It was his newfound discipline and emotional self-control. Rahm's tranquility didn't weaken his determination; it made him stronger and more resilient. He learned from his mistakes and didn't let them affect him negatively.

When Rahm missed a birdie putt, instead of getting frustrated, he acknowledged it as a good attempt. He had control over his golf swing and his emotions. This balance led him to victory at the U.S. Open.

Rahm's transformation and success show us the power of discipline and patience. His story is an inspiration for aspiring golfers and anyone striving to master self-control and discipline. Remember, even when faced with challenges and setbacks, with discipline and emotional self-control, you can overcome them and achieve great success, just like Jon Rahm did as the U.S. Open Champion.

## Teeing Up: Actionable Steps to Cultivate Discipline

**For Athletes:**

1. ***Understanding Discipline:*** It's important to grasp the concept of discipline and how it can improve your golf game. Recognize that consistent practice and a structured approach to learning are key to developing mental toughness.

2. ***Thinking Strategically:*** Cultivate strategic thinking skills and understand the power of small, consistent actions. Know that making steady improvements in your game over time can have a big impact.

3. ***Practicing Mindfulness:*** Engage in mindfulness practices to better understand your thoughts and emotions. This can help you stay focused on the course and improve your discipline.

4. ***Developing Routines:*** Establish routines that align

with your playing style. This will reinforce discipline and help you replace unproductive habits with beneficial ones.

5. ***Regular Analysis:*** Make it a habit to regularly analyze your performance. Identify areas for improvement and develop a disciplined practice plan to work on those areas.

Remember, discipline comes from consistent effort and practice. By incorporating these steps into your golfing routine, you will gradually build your mental toughness and see improvements in your performance on the course.

# Chapter 5

# Unshakeable Self-Belief

"Confidence is the 15th and most important club in the bag," Lydia Ko, the young golf prodigy, famously declared. This simple statement holds true not only in golf but also in life.

Lydia's journey is marked by her unwavering self-belief. Starting her professional career at a young age, she faced pressure, expectations, applause, and criticism. Throughout it all, her self-belief acted as her guiding light, leading her through challenges towards victory and acclaim.

In golf and in life, confidence and self-belief play a vital role. Golf is not just about physical skill but also about conquering the mind. When you stand on the green, it's not just the wind or the swing that affects you. It's that voice in your head, questioning your abilities and creating doubt.

Proactive confidence is key in this situation. It means taking control of your self-belief, rather than letting circumstances or external factors dictate it. When self-doubt arises, it's important to regain control, shift focus to the positive, and objectively evaluate your game.

Building confidence and self-belief takes time and effort. It's like constructing a skyscraper, where preparation forms the foundation. This includes perfecting your equipment, honing your skills, developing a strategic mindset, maintaining fitness, and building mental resilience. Consistency and discipline are the building blocks of this skyscraper of confidence.

The inspiring story of Jason Day's victory at the 2018 Wells Fargo tournament exemplifies the power of unshakeable self-belief. Overcoming self-doubt, he emerged victorious, showing us the importance of confidence in achieving success.

By the end of this chapter, you will understand that self-belief is a skill that can be developed. You will learn how to navigate self-doubt, the significance of preparation, and how to cultivate unshakeable confidence in your game. This will bring you closer to becoming an exceptional golfer.

### A Game of Confidence

When it comes to golf, confidence plays a significant role in determining a player's success. The game is not just about physical skills but also about mental fortitude. It's like a Game of Confidence, where players showcase their abilities on the course.

Confidence sets the great players apart from the average ones. To consistently perform well, a player must believe in their abilities. This unwavering belief acts as a shield, helping them stay resilient and focused even when faced with challenges. Instead of seeing missed shots as failures, confident golfers view them as opportunities to learn and improve.

However, self-doubt can hinder performance. It can arise before a swing or after a poor shot, undermining a golfer's abilities. Self-doubt triggers stress and anxiety, activating the fight-or-flight response that hampers fine motor skills. The body's physiological changes make it difficult to control movements and maintain focus.

Self-doubt can also lead to the subconscious mind taking over. The mind responds to perceived threats as if facing physical danger, limiting conscious control. To manage self-doubt and foster confidence, golfers can use proven techniques to focus their attention, relax their bodies, and calm their nerves. By doing so, they can access the memory centers that facilitate their best swings and strokes.

Confidence in golf goes beyond executing good shots; it encompasses feeling positive about your game overall. It's about having faith in your abilities, trusting your decisions, and reacting well to both good and bad performances. Confidence acts as a golfer's mental armor, enabling them to perform their best, even under pressure.

So, remember that confidence is not just about playing well but also feeling good about your game. Develop your confidence and watch your golf skills soar to new heights!

**Proactive vs. Reactive Confidence**

Confidence is like a superpower that can make a huge difference in your performance, both in golf and in life. There are two types of confidence: proactive and reactive.

Proactive confidence is when you believe in yourself no matter what happens. Great athletes like Jordan Spieth have proactive confidence. They have a strong foundation of self-belief built on positive experiences and hard work. Even if they have a small setback, it doesn't shake their confidence because they know they are capable.

On the other hand, reactive confidence is when your belief in yourself is easily influenced by small setbacks or what others say. It's like a rollercoaster ride where your confidence goes up and down based on how well you're doing or what people think of you.

Building and maintaining confidence is an ongoing process. It involves many things, like preparing well, knowing your strengths and weaknesses, getting good coaching, setting clear goals, and developing a positive mindset. It's about focusing on what you do well and learning from your mistakes. Confidence is not just important in golf but in every aspect of life, whether it's school, relationships, or pursuing your dreams. When you believe in yourself, you can achieve great things.

Remember, confidence is a skill that you can develop and improve over time. It's not about being perfect or always winning, but about having faith in yourself and bouncing back from setbacks. Building confidence is an investment in yourself that will benefit you in all areas of life. So, believe in yourself, stay positive, and watch how your confidence helps you reach new heights!

### What to Do When Self-Doubt Strikes

Self-doubt is something we all face at some point, and it's especially common in a sport like golf where the mental game is just as important as physical skills. When self-doubt clouds your mind, it's important to know how to navigate through it. Here are some helpful tips:

Avoid the All or Nothing Mindset: It's easy to think that winning is the only measure of success and that losing means you've failed. But in reality, every performance has its positives and learning opportunities. Instead of being too hard on yourself, focus on the things you did well, even if the outcome wasn't what you hoped for. Remember, even the best golfers have bad days. Embrace those moments as motivation to improve and keep growing.

Learn from Justin Thomas: Look at the example of golfers like Justin Thomas, who, despite not winning every tournament, find positives in their performance. Even when things don't go perfectly, they recognize that every shot is a chance to learn and get better. Remember that mistakes are part of the journey, and they help you improve and become a stronger player.

Embrace a Scale of Improvement: Instead of thinking in black and white terms, rate your performance on a scale of 1 to 10. Not every day will be your best day, but there's always room for growth. Use each round as an opportunity to assess your progress and set new goals for improvement. Celebrate the small victories along the way.

Taming Self-Doubt in Golf: When self-doubt creeps in during a game, use it as a signal to heighten your focus. Instead of letting it hold you back, view it as an opportunity to step up your game. Challenge negative thoughts by reframing them into positive ones. For example, if you're worried about making a mistake, remind yourself of all the great shots you've made and believe in your ability to perform well. Use positive mantras, like "I CHOOSE TO FEEL NOW," to reinforce your confidence and focus.

Remember, self-doubt is normal, but it doesn't have to control you. By reframing your thoughts and focusing on the positive aspects of your game, you can overcome self-doubt and perform at your best. Use self-doubt as a signal to step up your focus and turn it into positive energy. With practice and a positive mindset, you can conquer self-doubt and achieve your goals on the golf course and in life.

### Take a Step Back

When you evaluate your performance, it's important to step back and look at the bigger picture. Sometimes, we get so caught up in one shot or one game that we forget about our overall progress. Instead of dwelling on the outcome of a single moment, reflect on your performance over time. Look for patterns and areas where you can improve. By doing this, you can identify the source of your self-doubt and focus on the right areas for growth.

**Choose How You Feel**

When self-doubt and negative thoughts arise, you have the power to choose how you respond to them. Instead of letting them consume you, recognize that these feelings are normal and even beneficial. Use them as motivation to push yourself further. Focus on your target and visualize where you want the ball to go. Be fully present in the moment, feeling the club in your hands, the ground beneath your feet, and the wind on your face. By channeling your awareness into hitting the perfect shot, you can overcome self-doubt and perform at your best.

**Embrace the Learning Experience**

Remember that golf is not just a physical game but a mental one as well. Dealing with self-doubt is about understanding and reshaping your thoughts. Focus on the positives and choose to respond to negative feelings in a productive way. Every shot, every round, and every game is an opportunity to learn and grow. Embrace them all, and you'll see your confidence soar with each swing.

By stepping back, choosing how you feel, and embracing the learning experience, you can overcome self-doubt and unlock your full potential on the golf course. Keep practicing, stay positive, and watch your confidence grow, one swing at a time.

**How to Build Confidence and Self-Belief**

Embarking on the journey of golf, you'll discover the treasure of self-confidence and belief. Jack Nicklaus, a golf legend, said, "Confidence is believing in your own ability, knowing what you have to do to win. My confidence was developed through preparation." Let's explore the stepping stones to nurturing this self-belief through preparation.

### Equipment Needs

Equip yourself for success with the right gear. From clubs that match your swing to weather-appropriate attire, having the essentials boosts your confidence on the field. Your golf bag should be like a treasure chest, filled with balls, tees, a rangefinder, towel, extra glove, and even first aid items. Your equipment is your trusted companion, ready to support you through every hole.

### Technical Skills

Mastering your swing, understanding the ball's lie, reading the greens, and setting up correctly are essential. A reliable pre-shot routine brings stability to your game, making you feel in control. This mastery empowers you with the confidence to face any challenge on the course.

### Strategic Approach

Success in golf is not just about getting the ball in the hole, but doing so with the fewest strokes. Prepare by formulating a solid plan for each course you play. Consider the conditions, weather, and hole layouts. The more adept you are at the strategic side of golf, the more confident you'll feel on the green.

### Physical Preparedness

Are you physically fit for the game? Do you have a warm-up routine before each round? Good nutrition and hydration are also important. Knowing your physical abilities and preparing accordingly can make a significant difference in your confidence and performance.

### Mindset and Visualization

Your mindset is crucial. Maintaining a positive attitude, being ready for different emotions on the course, and visualizing successful shots are essential for mental preparation. Confidence is the belief in your ability to succeed, and visualizing success can strengthen that belief.

### Cultivate Patience

Golf requires patience and composure. Learning to handle frustration effectively can increase your confidence over time. Remember that golf takes time to master. Embrace each step of your journey, and don't rush the process.

### Establish Routines

Routines create consistency and predictability, boosting confidence. Whether it's a pre-shot routine or a specific practice routine, familiar patterns create a comfort zone. Embrace your routine, knowing that each step leads to becoming a more confident golfer.

### Embrace Your Unique Playing Style

Celebrate your unique swing and playing style. Don't feel pressured to change it to fit a mold. Embracing your uniqueness makes the game more enjoyable and builds your confidence as you appreciate your abilities.

### Keep Learning and Improving

No matter how skilled you become, there's always room for improvement. Stay open-minded and willing to learn new techniques or strategies. This continuous growth improves your game and increases confidence. Remember, every champion was once a learner.

By following these steps, you can build confidence and self-belief on your golfing journey. Prepare, practice, and believe in yourself. With each swing, your confidence will soar, propelling you to new heights in the game of golf.

### The Need for Mental Fortitude in Golf

When you step onto the fairway, you face various challenges, regardless of your experience level. Sometimes, you may get nervous on the first tee or find yourself overthinking your swing. It's easy to get caught up in technical details and forget the true essence of the game: having fun, being creative, and enjoying the moment. This tendency can create unnecessary tension and hinder your performance.

### Meditation: A Tool for Mental Strength

Meditation can be a powerful tool to overcome these challenges. However, it's important to understand that meditation is not just about relaxation. It helps cultivate mental strength and resilience.

Practicing meditation allows you to center your mind, promoting calmness, relaxation, and focus. These qualities have a significant impact on your performance on the course.

### Activating Confidence Through Meditation

Confidence is not solely based on how well you perform. It stems from believing in your abilities and knowing you can improve. Meditation plays a crucial role in activating confidence.

By visualizing successful shots and positive outcomes during meditation, you reinforce your self-belief and activate confidence. Regular meditation helps embed these images in your mind, becoming a source of self-assurance.

### Cultivating Control With Meditation

Meditation also helps nurture control on the golf course. Being in control of your thoughts and emotions is vital to staying in the zone. Like deep breathing exercises, meditation aids in developing this control. It encourages you to let go of conscious judgment and focus on the game at hand.

### Responding Positively to Mistakes

Bouncing back from mistakes can be challenging for golfers. It often stems from a lack of mental resilience. Regular meditation can help you respond positively to mistakes, accept them, and concentrate on the next shot. Meditation fosters a "present-moment" mindset, freeing you from past errors and future anxieties. It enables a constructive recovery from setbacks and cultivates a resilient mental approach to the game.

Embracing meditation can significantly enhance your mental prowess and improve your performance on the course. It builds mental strength, activates confidence, and cultivates control—essential qualities for a successful golfer. So, whether you're a teen starting your golfing journey or a parent looking to elevate your teen's game, consider incorporating meditation into your training regime for a holistic approach to golf.

Remember, preparation isn't just about having the right clubs. It's also about having the right mindset. Confidence is not something you're born with; it's something you develop through thorough preparation. Embrace this comprehensive preparation to gain a realistic understanding of effective golf and the confidence to play the best game of your life.

### Stories to Inspire: Saving the Day

In the thrilling world of professional golf, the toughest opponent isn't always the course or the other players—it's often the battle that rages inside your own head. Just ask Jason Day, a talented golfer known for his focus and precision. But even he faced a formidable foe: self-doubt.

It was the final day of the 2018 Wells Fargo tournament, and Day found himself in a tough spot. He was missing fairways, making mistakes, and doubts started creeping into his mind. It seemed like everything was falling apart. But here's where the story takes an exciting turn.

Instead of giving in to his insecurities, Day decided to face them head-on. He admitted that he was battling demons inside his head, but he didn't let them consume him. He knew he had to push through and keep going. It was a moment of strength and determination.

Day chose to focus on his short game, the part of his game that was working well that day. And guess what? It paid off big time. Despite his struggles on the green, he found redemption and strength in his short game. It was like his secret weapon, saving his day and maybe even the whole tournament.

With incredible resilience and mental toughness, Day birdied two of the final three holes, securing a remarkable victory at the Wells Fargo Championship.

This inspiring story shows us the power of a positive mind-set. Even when faced with challenges and self-doubt, Day was able to turn his performance around. He didn't change anything external—he changed his perspective. He focused on what was going right instead of dwelling on what was going wrong.

We all have moments of doubt and uncertainty, just like Day. But when those moments come, remember that the battle is often in your mind. By focusing on the positives, you can boost your confidence and resilience. Day's story proves that the battle of the mind is one you can win—with perseverance, focus, and a positive outlook.

Whether you're facing the tough greens of a golf course or the ups and downs of everyday life, this lesson holds true. Believe in yourself, stay positive, and never underestimate the power of saving the day with the strength of your own mind.

## Teeing Up: Actionable Steps to Cultivate Unshakeable Self-Belief

*For the Athlete*
    1. *Understand Confidence:* Embrace the concept of

confidence and its impact on your golf performance. Recognize the detrimental effects of self-doubt and work toward eliminating it.

2. ***Develop Emotional Control:*** Learn to manage your emotions, especially when self-doubt strikes. Analyze your performance objectively and focus on overall progress rather than isolated instances.

3. ***Create a Positive Mantra:*** Establish a personal positive mantra that you can use to shift focus from negativity and self-doubt. This mantra can be a source of motivation and a tool to regain focus.

4. ***Trust Yourself:*** Cultivate trust in your abilities. Understand that trust is a manifestation of self-belief and that doubting your abilities can inhibit your performance.

5. ***Engage in Regular Practice:*** Incorporate consistent practice into your routine. Regular practice is key to refining your skills, preparing your mind for challenges, and, ultimately, boosting your confidence.

Remember, confidence and self-belief are not innate traits but skills that can be developed. The above steps can aid in fostering an unshakeable belief in yourself, enabling you to thrive even under pressure. Embrace the journey of self-belief, and enjoy the transformation it brings to your golf game.

# Chapter 6

# Goal Setting: Aim High, Swing Strong

I magine yourself standing on the lush green fairway, just like golf champion Rory McIlroy. He's not only focused on winning tournaments but also on the journey that gets him there—setting the right goals. Goals that are like stepping stones leading to your ultimate golfing dreams.

Goals are like maps, guiding us on our golfing adventures. They help us stay on track, measure our progress, and push ourselves to new heights. But remember, setting the right goals is key. They should align with your abilities, aspirations, and the reality around you.

McIlroy's wisdom goes beyond the golf course. Setting un-realistic goals or chasing things you don't truly want can lead to frustration. It's like trying to hit a hole-in-one on every shot—it's just not practical. Instead, we'll explore the SMART framework—a secret formula that ensures your goals are Specific, Measurable, Attainable, Realistic, and Time-sensitive.

In this chapter, we'll learn to balance short-term wins with long-term dreams. We'll discover the importance of holding ourselves accountable and the power of setting goals that are not only meaningful but also within our control.

Drawing inspiration from another golf champion, Justin Thomas, we'll see how setting personal, motivating goals can transform our game. But remember, your journey is unique. It's not about following someone else's path, but about creating your own golfing adventure.

So, let's dive into this chapter and uncover the art of setting the right goals. Together, we'll learn to aim high, swing strong, and unleash our full potential in every swing of life. As McIlroy said, "I can't control winning a tournament... I'd rather set goals that are objective and measurable, that I'm in control of." Get ready to chart your course to greatness!

### **Goals and Golf**

Goals in golf are like targets in life. You can't hit a hole-in-one without a hole to aim for, and you can't make progress without clear goals. Setting goals is about looking beyond the task at hand and focusing on the bigger picture.

Goals in golf, just like in life, come in different shapes and sizes. Let's explore a few of them:

- Technical Goals: These are like refining your golf swing or mastering a new stroke. In life, this could mean learning a new skill or getting better at something you already do.

- Target Goals: In golf, this might mean aiming for a specific score in your next tournament. In your personal or professional life, it could be aiming for a promotion or maintaining a good grade point average in school.

- Future Goals: These are long-term goals, like winning a national championship or attending your dream university.

Setting goals isn't just about making a wish list. It's also about prioritizing your goals based on their importance. This helps you manage your time, develop routines, and establish good habits. The bigger the goal, the more time and effort it may require.

Setting the right goals can have a big impact on how you feel. If a goal seems impossible to reach, it can make you feel like a failure. But if a goal doesn't really matter to you, it can leave you feeling unmotivated. The trick is finding the sweet spot—setting goals that challenge and excite you, while still being achievable. Remember, hitting a hole-in-one in golf is amazing but rare. Instead, focus on making steady progress with each swing.

Golf and life have a lot in common. Both require patience, perseverance, and precision. They reward those who take calculated risks and understand the power of focus and de-termination. So, as you make your way across the golf course and through life, remember that every swing, every hole, and every game is an opportunity to learn, grow, and get better. It's not about being perfect, but about striving for continual improvement.

### The Power of Setting the Right Goals

Did you know that setting goals can have a big impact on how you feel? It's true! When we set goals that are impossible to reach, it can make us feel like we've failed. And if we set goals that don't really matter to us, it can leave us feeling un-motivated. That's why it's important to find the right balance.

The key is to set goals that are both challenging and achiev-able. These goals should excite us and push us to do our best. Just like hitting a hole-in-one in golf is amazing but rare, it's more realistic and rewarding to focus on making steady progress with each swing.

Setting the right goals not only affects our performance in golf but also in life. Both golf and life require patience, perseverance, and precision. They reward those who take calculated risks and understand the power of focus and determination. So, as you make your way through the golf course and through life, remember that every swing, every hole, and every game is an opportunity to learn, grow, and get better.

It's important to know that neither golf nor life is about being perfect. It's about striving for continual improvement. So, set goals that challenge and excite you, and remember to enjoy the journey. With each step, you'll become stronger, more confident, and ready to take on any challenge that comes your way.

### Setting SMART Goals: A Path to Success

Let's dive deeper into the world of goal-setting and discover how it can transform your approach to achieving your dreams, not just in sports or golf, but in all areas of your life—academics, relationships, personal growth, and more.

SMART is an acronym that stands for Specific, Measurable, Attainable, Realistic, and Time-sensitive. Let's break it down and see how each element plays a crucial role in setting effective goals.

Specific: Be clear about what you want to achieve. Vague ideas won't get you far. For example, saying "I want to get better at math" is not specific. Instead, make it something like, "I want to score at least 90% on my next math test." This way, you have a clear direction and a target to aim for.

Measurable: Make your goal something you can track and measure. Being able to see your progress and know when you've achieved your goal is important. For instance, instead of saying you want to improve your math skills, set a specific score target for your next test. This allows you to measure your success along the way.

Attainable: Goals should challenge you, but they should also be within reach. Setting unrealistic goals can lead to frustration. If you're currently scoring around 70% on your math tests, aiming for a 95% score in the next month may be too high. Start with a goal of reaching 80%, which is challenging but attainable.

Realistic: Goals should align with your abilities and resources. Setting goals that are too far-fetched can set you up for disappointment. Consider your current situation and what you can realistically achieve. This way, you'll stay motivated and confident in your ability to reach your goals.

Time-sensitive: Give your goals a deadline. Setting a timeline creates a sense of urgency and helps you stay focused. Without a deadline, it's easy to keep pushing your goals off. For example, you can say, "I will achieve an 80% score on my next math test in four weeks." This sets a clear target to work towards.

Now, let's put it all into action:

*1. Decide what you want to accomplish:* Clearly define your goal, whether it's academic success, improving in sports, or personal development.

*2. Establish immediate and future objectives:* Set targets for the near future, like the upcoming weeks or months, as well as long-term goals that may take years to achieve. Make sure your immediate objectives contribute to your long-term aspirations.

*3. Write down your goals and hold yourself accountable:* Putting your goals on paper makes them tangible. Regularly reviewing them will keep you motivated and remind you of your commitments. Share your goals with someone you trust, like a friend or family member, who can support and encourage you along the way.

Remember, goal-setting is not set in stone. If your circumstances change, don't be afraid to revise your goals. Stay flexible and open-minded as you work towards your aspirations. The SMART framework is a powerful tool for breaking down big goals into manageable steps. By following this approach, you can set clear, achievable targets and make steady progress towards your dreams.

## The Right Goals for You: A Personalized Approach

As a golfer (or parent of a golfer), it's important to understand that goal-setting should be tailored to you. What works for someone else may not work for you. The "right" goals are the ones that align with your skills, interests, and long-term aspirations. They should be challenging yet achievable, pushing you to grow without becoming overwhelming or discouraging. Setting the right goals requires understanding your abilities and what you genuinely want to achieve.

### Process vs. Outcome

In golf, goals can be divided into two main types: process goals and outcome/results goals.

Process Goals: These goals focus on the steps or procedures necessary for improvement. They aren't directly tied to winning or specific results but are crucial for enhancing performance. For example, a process goal could be practicing your short game three days a week or using speed training sticks regularly. Process goals are within your control and help relieve pressure by focusing on effort and learning.

Outcome Goals: These goals are directly tied to the results you want to achieve. They include winning tournaments or achieving a specific score. While outcome goals can provide motivation, they can also be influenced by external factors. To balance them, it's helpful to set process goals that guide your daily actions and make your outcome goals more attainable.

Practice Goals: These goals optimize your training sessions. They involve specific tasks to improve your skills, such as making a certain number of putts each week or dedicating more time to your short game. Consistent, focused practice is key to improving your abilities.

On-Course Goals: These goals focus on enhancing your performance during actual play. They can include mental strategies like positive self-talk or physical routines like following a pre-shot routine. On-course goals are aimed at improving your strategies and maintaining focus and composure on the course.

### Goals NOT to Aim For

While setting goals is important, it's crucial to avoid vague or non-specific goals that are hard to measure or attain. Examples include wanting to "drive it longer" or "play more consistently." Instead, choose goals like "average 275 yards off the tee" or "hit 50% of greens with my 4-6 irons." Clear and measurable goals provide a target to aim for.

Setting goals can revolutionize your game, motivating you to continually improve. Whether they're process, outcome, practice, or on-course goals, they provide a roadmap for your progress. Just remember to make them specific, measurable, attainable, realistic, and time-bound (SMART) to ensure their effectiveness. As you or your teen embark on this journey, remember that progress is a process, and every small step towards your goals is a victory in itself.

### Stories to Inspire: How Justin Thomas Sets Goals

Justin Thomas, the famous professional golfer, has an interesting habit that gets everyone talking: he sets his goals for the season and keeps them to himself until the season ends. This might seem strange, but it shows how much Thomas understands the power of personal goals and how they can motivate us. Growing up in a golf-loving family, Thomas inherited his strong dedication from his father, a respected PGA professional. But along with his unwavering dedication, Thomas has a secret weapon that helps him succeed on the golf course: his list of goals.

In today's digital world, Thomas keeps track of his goals using the notes app on his phone. Before each season, he carefully writes down his objectives, whether it's about improving his swing or winning a certain number of tournaments. But here's the twist: he keeps these goals to himself until the season is over. Then, he looks back and evaluates his performance, checking off the goals he achieved and reflecting on the ones he didn't. Even if he sees a red "X" next to some goals, showing they weren't reached, he's still proud of his efforts.

Thomas's approach inspires teenagers and parents alike to set specific goals. Short-term goals could be about improving swing mechanics or mastering bunker shots. Long-term goals, like Thomas's, might involve winning tournaments or achieving a specific scoring average. But it's important to remember that goal setting is personal and unique to each individual. One person might aim to hit 14 greens in regulation every round, while another might find joy in simply enjoying the game. Both are valid, and both can motivate us and help us progress.

Thomas's story reminds us that it's okay if we don't reach all our goals. What matters is the journey, the effort we put in, and the personal growth we experience along the way. Goals are meant to ignite motivation, encourage persistence, and open doors to new objectives.

Thomas, the winner of the 2022 PGA Championship, shows us how setting personal goals can lead to incredible success. But more importantly, he teaches us that goal setting is about self-improvement and personal satisfaction, not just about impressing others. In the end, it's you who stands over the ball, ready to take your shot.

## Teeing Up: Actionable Steps to Set the Right Goals

**For the Athlete:**

1. *Unlock the Power of Goals:* Discover how goals can guide your golf journey, shaping your skills and progress on the course.

2. *Use the SMART Framework:* When setting goals, make them Specific, Measurable, Attainable, Realistic, and Time-sensitive. This smart approach helps you set meaningful targets that you can actually achieve.

3. *Prioritize Your Goals:* Sort your goals by importance to manage your time and habits effectively, ensuring you focus on what matters most.

4. *Put It in Writing:* Solidify your commitment by writing down your goals. This simple act boosts your accountability and concentration.

5. *Process and Outcome Goals:* Learn the difference between process goals that improve your technique and outcome goals that focus on the end results. Both types are vital for your overall performance.

Remember, goal setting is not a one-time task, but an ongoing process that demands revisiting and refining. Embrace this process, and take comfort in the knowledge that the effort you put into setting the right goals can significantly shape your journey in golf. Enjoy the journey, and may each swing take you closer to your goals.

1.

2.

3.

4.

5.

6.

7.

8.

9.

10.

# Chapter 7

# Patience and Persistence

"E xecute, execute, execute..." The words reverberate through the air, carrying the wisdom of professional golfer J. L. Lewis. But it's more than just a command—it's a way of life. Golf teaches us that success isn't just about winning or losing; it's about making ourselves better with every stroke we take.

To truly understand this philosophy, let's dive into the career of J. L. Lewis, a golfer known for his unwavering resolve and quiet patience. He understood the value of looking beyond immediate challenges and adopting a long-term perspective. This mindset forms the foundation of mental toughness. In this chapter, we'll explore Lewis's journey and learn how it embodies the sixth skill we'll be focusing on: patience and persistence.

In golf, patience is crucial. It's the thread that weaves itself into every aspect of the game, affecting our swing, shots, and how we handle tough situations. Patience gives us the rhythm to persist when things don't go our way and fuels our growth and improvement. It separates those who give up from those who keep going.

Consider the story of Jordan Spieth, a phenomenal player whose impatience led to a decline in his score. It's a powerful example of how patience—or the lack of it—can impact our game. Practicing is pointless if we're not willing to do it over and over again. Cultivating patience requires discipline, emotional self-control, and remembering why we play golf in the first place. It means showing up, even when faced with challenges.

Equally important to patience is persistence. The journey of golf, and life, is filled with ups and downs. Mental toughness, built through patience and persistence, allows us to endure and adapt to these fluctuations. It gives us the strength to keep going, not because it's easy, but because it's hard.

Throughout this chapter, we'll explore inspiring stories like that of Michael Thompson, who exemplifies extraordinary patience. Thompson focused on minimizing mistakes rather than seeking perfection with every shot. His story highlights the power of patience and persistence, proving that these qualities pave the path to victory on and off the course.

Join us on this journey in Chapter 7 as we embrace the beauty of patience and the virtue of persistence. Discover the secrets of resilience and mental toughness. Remember, it's all about "Execute, execute, execute..."—one shot, one stroke, one step at a time.

### How Patience Affects Your Game

There's an old saying that "golf is a game of inches." But more than that, it's a game that teaches us the importance of patience. Golf isn't just about skill and strategy—it's about having the patience to stay calm and focused throughout the entire game. Whether you're facing a challenging bunker shot or feeling nervous about being in the lead, patience can make all the difference in how well you play.

For beginner players, golf can be overwhelming. There's so much to learn, from the rules to the techniques, and it can feel like a lot to take in. But it's patience that helps you see beyond the initial struggles and embrace the learning process. With every swing, you have the opportunity to grow and improve.

Patience is essential not only in practice but also in executing your shots during a game. Practice isn't just about repetition—it's about building resilience. It's about being patient and persistent, even when the results don't seem to be going your way. As a golfer, you need the patience to keep working on refining your shots and enhancing your overall game.

Patience also plays a crucial role in making smart decisions on the course. When faced with challenging situations like a bunker shot, patience helps you avoid making rushed and impulsive choices. It gives you the mental clarity to evaluate your options, think strategically, and find the best way to navigate out of tough spots. Patience affects not only your swing but also your overall game management, influencing how you handle difficult situations, maintain your rhythm, and deal with unexpected obstacles.

Remember, golf is a game that rewards patience. Stay calm, stay focused, and trust in the process. With each shot, you have the chance to learn, adapt, and improve. Embrace the value of patience, and it will take your game to new heights.

### Lessons from the Pros: The Tale of Jordan Spieth

Sometimes, the best lessons come from real-life stories. Let's take a look at the remarkable journey of Jordan Spieth and how his experience at the Masters taught us the power of patience in golf.

Picture this: Jordan Spieth, one of the top golfers in the world, was on the verge of a historic victory at the Masters. He was leading the tournament and had his sights set on the ultimate prize. But then, something unexpected happened. His rhythm faltered, and he hit two bad shots that threw him off balance. In that crucial moment, Spieth's patience was put to the test.

Unfortunately, Spieth let his impatience get the best of him. He rushed his putts and made costly mistakes. The lead slipped away, and so did his chance of winning the tournament. It was a tough lesson to learn, but it taught us all a valuable truth: Patience can make or break a game.

If Spieth had been more patient, if he had taken a step back and stayed calm, the outcome might have been different. Patience is not just important during practice or when facing challenges. It's especially vital when you're under pressure, when the stakes are high, and everything is on the line.

Spieth's story serves as a powerful reminder that patience is a game-changer. It's the key to maintaining composure, making wise decisions, and staying focused even when things don't go according to plan. It's about trusting in your abilities, being resilient, and believing that your time will come.

So, the next time you're out on the golf course, remember the tale of Jordan Spieth. Embrace the power of patience in every swing and every moment. Stay calm, stay focused, and let your patience guide you to victory.

**How to Nurture Patience in Golf**

Patience is like a muscle that needs to be strengthened and nurtured. Here are some strategies to help you develop and cultivate patience in your golf game:

1. Be aware of your triggers: Take note of what situations or outcomes make you feel impatient. Is it a missed putt or a bad shot? By identifying these triggers, you can mentally

prepare yourself to manage them better next time. Stay calm and composed, and don't let one mistake define your entire game.

2. Adopt a forward-looking mindset: Remember that golf is a marathon, not a sprint. Instead of dwelling on past mistakes, focus on the present moment and the remaining holes. Each shot is an opportunity for redemption and improvement. Embrace the learning process and let go of perfectionism.

3. Stick to a steady routine: Avoid rushing or making impulsive decisions on the course. Establish a consistent pace and rhythm in your game. Take your time to analyze your shots, plan your strategy, and execute with precision. A steady routine helps maintain your focus and keeps your mind calm and patient.

4. Embrace imperfection: Golf teaches us that perfection is elusive. Accept that mistakes will happen and use them as learning opportunities. Embrace the challenges and setbacks, knowing that they contribute to your growth as a golfer. Cultivate a mindset of resilience and perseverance.

Remember, building patience is not a one-time effort but an ongoing practice. Be patient with yourself as you work on developing this valuable skill. By nurturing patience in your golf game, you'll not only enhance your performance on the course but also cultivate a valuable life skill that can benefit you in many aspects of your journey.

### Patience and Persistence: Building a Strong Mindset

Imagine building a fortress of mental strength with two cornerstone virtues: patience and persistence. They may seem simple, but they hold incredible power. Let's explore how they work together to help you overcome challenges and achieve your goals.

Patience is like a wise mentor, teaching you the art of waiting and delayed gratification. It requires discipline and focus, reminding you that good things take time. Just as an athlete starts with the basics before reaching the elite level, patience is the foundation for success in any endeavor. It's a skill that needs nurturing, especially during the teenage years when everything seems urgent.

Persistence is the unstoppable force that keeps you moving forward, even when things get tough. Picture yourself in a dark tunnel. Persistence is the unwavering belief that there's light at the end, guiding you to take one step after another. It's the voice that whispers, "Don't give up." With persistence, setbacks become stepping stones, and obstacles become opportunities for growth.

These two virtues are partners in your journey. Patience asks you to wait for the right moment, while persistence pushes you to keep going. They complement each other, creating a powerful synergy. Life is full of ups and downs, and the road to personal development is no exception. Patience and persistence help you navigate the twists and turns, celebrating victories and overcoming setbacks.

Motivation is like a spark that ignites your fire, but patience and persistence are the fuel that keep it burning. When motivation wanes, they provide the strength to keep going. They keep you grounded, reminding you of your goals and the value of perseverance.

Patience and persistence are the endurance athletes of your mental toolbox. They may not be flashy, but they are indispensable. They steady your focus, provide discipline during life's storms, and prove your resilience. By exercising these traits consistently, you build mental muscle and equip yourself to face challenges head-on.

These virtues are like unwavering lighthouses, guiding you through the stormy seas of life. Patience reminds you that great things take time, persistence shows you the way forward, and perspective keeps you on track. They're not just tools to be used in tough times; they're habits to be cultivated in your everyday life.

So, embrace patience and persistence as lifelong companions. Nurture them, for they will carry you through the highs and lows, helping you build mental toughness and achieve your dreams. Remember, success is not a sprint; it's a marathon. With patience and persistence, you'll reach the finish line and beyond.

### The Tale of Michael Thompson: The Power of Patience

In the thrilling world of professional golf, one golfer named Michael Thompson showed us the incredible strength of patience. He wasn't always a superstar, but he never gave up. Instead, he focused on playing a steady and smart game.

During the TPC Twin Cities tournament, Thompson amazed everyone with a flawless round. He hit all 18 greens and made some amazing putts. But it wasn't just luck. Thompson had a plan. He played it safe, sticking to his strengths in iron play and putting while being careful not to make mistakes.

Analyzing Thompson's performance with the help of advanced technology, we discovered that his iron play and putting skills were outstanding. He made very few mistakes compared to other players. That's because he had the patience to stay focused and make smart decisions on the course.

Thompson's strategy might not have been flashy or risky, but it worked. He showed us that being patient and playing to your strengths can lead to great success. And it paid off for him in a big way—he won the tournament!

So, what can we learn from Michael Thompson? Well, sometimes in golf, as in life, we need to take our time and make smart choices. It's easy to get caught up in trying to do something amazing with every shot, but patience is key. By staying patient, we can avoid making unnecessary mistakes and give ourselves the best chance to succeed.

Thompson's story reminds us that greatness comes to those who work hard, stay focused, and never give up. With patience and perseverance, we can achieve our goals, both on and off the golf course. So, the next time you're out there playing, remember to be patient, play smart, and let success come to you, just like it did for Michael Thompson.

## Teeing Up: Actionable Steps to Improve Mental Toughness

### For the Athlete

1. *Embrace the Journey:* Remember that golf is a long-term journey. Be patient with your progress and persistent in your practice. Understand that improvement may not be linear, and be prepared for ups and downs.

2. *Prioritize Consistency:* Show up for practice consistently. It's not about perfecting a skill in one session but rather about improving gradually over time.

3. *Emotional Self-Control:* Practice emotional self-control. When things seem to be going off the rails, take a step back, breathe, and be patient.

4. ***Identify Your Triggers:*** Recognize what makes you impatient on the course. Is it a missed shot, a high-stakes situation, or pressure from opponents? Once you're aware of these triggers, you can work on strategies to manage your reactions better.

5. ***Be Inspired:*** Take inspiration from Michael Thompson. His patience and strategy of minimizing mistakes rather than trying to hit every shot perfectly could be a helpful approach to emulate in your own game.

6.

7.

8.

9.

10.

# Chapter 8

# Learning to Embrace Failure: Bouncing Back Strong

I n the world of golf, failure is a common companion. Even the greatest golfers like Phil Mickelson, Jack Nicklaus, and Tiger Woods have experienced setbacks. But here's the secret—they didn't let failure define them. Instead, they used it as fuel to bounce back stronger.

Failure is not the end; it's a chance for growth. When we miss a putt or hit a bad shot, we learn valuable lessons. Failure shows us where we need to improve and helps us develop our skills. It's not something to be feared or embarrassed about, but rather embraced as a stepping stone to success.

To bounce back from failure, we need a powerful combination of self-awareness, goal-setting, and patience. We must understand why we failed, set realistic goals, and be patient with ourselves as we strive for improvement. It's a process that takes time, but it's worth it.

Take the inspiring journey of James Hahn. He faced setbacks and doubts, even giving up golf for a while. But he didn't let failure define him. Instead, he persevered and eventually achieved victory on the PGA Tour. His story teaches us that failure is not the end—it's an opportunity to rise above and achieve greatness.

In the rest of this chapter, we'll explore the depths of failure and its impact on our performance. It's not an easy topic, but an important one. As Phil Mickelson once said, failure is his greatest motivator. Let's use failure as a driving force to work harder, improve, and become better golfers and better individuals.

Remember, failure is not the end of the road—it's just a detour. Bounce back, learn from your mistakes, and keep swinging. Success is waiting for you on the other side of failure.

## **The Truth About Failure**

The truth about failure is that it's a part of everyone's journey, even for the greatest athletes. In golf, players like Rory McIlroy, Tiger Woods, and Bubba Watson have all faced their fair share of failures. McIlroy had a tough year where he didn't perform as well as he wanted to. Tiger Woods went through a period without winning a major championship. And Bubba Watson struggled to regain his winning form after his Masters victory.

But here's what's important: it's not the failure itself that defines a person, but how they respond to it. It's about bouncing back, learning from mistakes, and showing resilience. Failure is an opportunity for growth, a chance to become even better. It's in these moments of setback that true character and greatness are forged.

So, remember, everyone fails. It's a normal part of the journey. What matters is how you respond to failure and keep moving forward. Use it as a stepping stone towards success, and you'll come out stronger on the other side.

**Fear and Failure are Connected**

Let's explore the connection between failure and fear a little deeper. Many golfers, and people in general, are scared of failing. They worry about not being good enough, making mistakes, or looking foolish in front of others. This fear can hold them back and stop them from taking risks that could help them grow and get better.

One reason for this fear is something called the Spotlight Effect. It's when we believe that everyone is watching and judging us more harshly than they actually are. This makes us feel even more self-conscious and afraid of failing. But here's the thing: most people are actually more focused on themselves than on what others are doing. Realizing this can help us overcome our fear of failure and feeling silly.

When we change how we see failure, something amazing happens. Instead of seeing it as a terrible thing to avoid at all costs, we start to view it as a chance to learn and grow. Failure becomes a stepping-stone on our journey to improvement and success. It's not the end of the road, but a valuable experience that helps us become better. This new perspective empowers us to be more resilient, determined, and successful in golf and in life.

So, remember, failure and fear are connected, but we have the power to change how we think about them. Embrace failure as a part of the learning process, and don't let fear hold you back. Take risks, make mistakes, and use them as opportunities to grow. You'll be amazed at what you can achieve when you let go of the fear of failure.

**Why we *NEED* failure in sports**

In the world of golf, failure is an inseparable part of the game. It's a reminder that even the best golfers face challenges and setbacks. But why is failure so important? Why do all golfers need to experience it? Well, failure is a powerful teacher that guides us towards improvement. It shows us where our weaknesses lie and where we need to focus our efforts. Without failure, we may never truly understand our areas for growth.

How we perceive failure is crucial. It can either bring us down or lift us up. If we let failure defeat us, it can lead to self-doubt and frustration. But if we embrace failure as a learning opportunity, it becomes a catalyst for progress and skill development. Failure keeps us grounded and reminds us that there's always room for improvement.

Success, on the other hand, can sometimes be misleading. It may be due to luck rather than skill. Failure helps us differentiate between luck and true mastery. It pushes us to analyze our mistakes and make the necessary corrections, leading to more consistent success. Failure becomes a valuable time machine that allows us to learn from the past and shape a better future.

In golf and in life, failure is not the end. It's a chance to rise stronger and wiser. Embracing failure with acceptance and resilience helps us bounce back faster. It teaches us to let go of past mistakes and focus on our future potential. These lessons extend beyond the golf course, shaping our mindset in all areas of life.

So, as a golfer, remember that every missed shot, every bad round is an opportunity for growth. Failure is not a defeat but a stepping stone towards becoming your best self. Embrace it, learn from it, and let it guide you to success.

**How to Conquer Failure**

Now that we know failure is a part of the game that every golfer must face, how can we conquer failure and turn it into an opportunity for growth? Here are some strategies used by pro golfers that can help young athletes navigate the challenges of failure with resilience and grace.

First, recognize that failure in golf is specific. A missed putt or a bad drive doesn't define your entire game. It's just one aspect that needs improvement. Use each failure as a chance to learn and grow, focusing on the areas that need attention.

Next, unearth the roots of failure. Understand that some factors are beyond your control, like the unpredictable nature of the course. Embrace the challenges and adapt to them. Instead of trying to control everything, tune into your environment and adjust accordingly.

Set realistic goals that inspire progress. Know your capabilities and set targets that stretch your abilities without setting yourself up for inevitable failure. Keep your goals flexible, allowing room for growth and celebrating small, incremental improvements along the way.

Don't forget to celebrate your strengths. While working on your weaknesses is important, playing to your strengths can give you an edge. Balance out your shortcomings by utilizing your assets and leveraging them to your advantage.

Remember the three pillars of Patience, Persistence, and Practice, also known as the three P's. Give yourself the patience to fail and learn from those failures. Be persistent in your efforts, even when progress seems slow. And practice deliberately, repeating the skills and strategies that need improvement.

Conquering failure is not an easy task, but it is a rewarding one. Every golfer faces failure, but it's how you respond that sets you apart. Embrace failure as a part of the game, knowing that it's an opportunity for growth. By adopting these strategies, young golfers can navigate the trials of the game with resilience and grace. Remember, the ability to conquer failure is like a hidden club in your golf bag, ready to be used when things don't go as planned. The challenge is not in avoiding failure but in learning how to dance with it and come out stronger on the other side.

### **Inspiring Story: James Hahn**

Let's dive into the inspiring story of James Hahn, whose journey from selling designer shoes to standing on the greens is a testament to resilience and pursuing one's dreams against all odds.

After completing his studies at Cal-Berkeley, Hahn embarked on various career paths, including real estate and marketing. While these jobs sustained him financially, they couldn't fulfill his deep passion for golf. Working at Nordstrom, Hahn's infectious personality and hard work earned him admiration from colleagues and customers, but his dream of playing golf remained on hold.

A turning point came when Hahn's former college golf teammates won the NCAA championship, an event he had missed out on. Determined not to let his past define his future, Hahn made a bold decision. Despite financial constraints, he left his job and returned to selling shoes at Nordstrom, which provided him with the income and flexibility to pursue his golfing dreams.

Hahn's journey back to golf was not easy. He spent years playing in different countries and tours before finally achieving victory. His infectious "Gangnam Style" dance after winning went viral and put him back in the spotlight.

Throughout his journey, Hahn's work ethic, positive attitude, and authentic self remained his greatest assets. Despite his success, he stays humble and appreciative of the challenges he faced along the way. Hahn's story is a reminder that it's never too late to chase your dreams and that success often comes from taking unconventional paths.

His resilience, hard work, and dedication serve as an inspiration to both young athletes and their parents. Hahn's story shows that setbacks and detours can lead to greater achievements and that staying true to yourself is key to finding fulfillment and happiness in life.

So, remember James Hahn's remarkable journey when faced with obstacles. Stay true to your dreams, work hard, and embrace the twists and turns that life throws your way. Success may not come in a straight line, but with determination and resilience, you can overcome any challenge and reach new heights.

## Teeing Up: Actionable Steps to Improve Mental Toughness

### *For the Athlete*

1. *Embrace Failure:* Understand that every golfer, including the pros, fails. Rather than fearing failure, use it as a means to improve.

2. *Learn from Failure:* Each failure provides valuable lessons about your game. Use these lessons to work on your weaknesses and refine your strengths.

3. *Identify the Cause:* When failure occurs, analyze the factors that led to it, including those beyond your control. This understanding will enable you to devise strategies to handle similar situations in the future.

4. *Set Realistic Goals:* Having achievable and realistic goals can help you manage failure. Revisit your goals regularly and adjust them based on your progress and performance.

5. *Balance Patience with Persistence:* Remember that improving your game is a process that requires both patience and persistence. Allow yourself room to fail, but also remain dedicated to your practice and continuous improvement.

# Chapter 9

# Practicing Positivity!

I n this chapter, we'll explore the incredible power of positivity and its impact on both golf and life. Let's dive in and discover how positivity can make a real difference in your game.

You may have heard the inspiring words of Jordan Spieth, a golfing legend who emphasizes the importance of embracing and enjoying the game. Even when facing difficult shots or challenging holes, staying positive is crucial. Spieth himself experienced a slump in his career but maintained a resilient mindset and focused on the positive aspects of his game. This led to a remarkable comeback and showcased the incredible mental strength required in golf.

Now, let's bust a few myths about positivity. First, positivity doesn't mean ignoring the negatives or pretending they don't exist. It's about embracing challenges and learning from them. Second, positive thinking isn't about completely eradicating negative thoughts. Instead, it's about interpreting them in a constructive way and maintaining an objective approach.

Positivity plays a significant role in golf because it helps calm your mind, shapes your overall mindset, and influences how you approach the game. When you have a positive outlook, it boosts your vision, enhances your focus, and leads to better performance. On the other hand, negative thinking can hinder your game and take away the enjoyment of playing.

So, how can you practice positivity? Here are some tips. Start by setting your intentions before the game, focusing on what you want to achieve. Visualize success and believe in yourself, as this boosts your confidence. Even when negative emotions arise, use them as opportunities for reflection and improvement.

One golfer who exemplifies the power of positivity is Ally McDonald. Despite battling negative thoughts and self-doubt, she harnessed the strength of positive thinking to secure a victory. Her story shows us firsthand how positivity can transform our performance.

The goal of this chapter is to inspire you, highlight the incredible power of positivity, and provide you with the tools to apply it to your game and life. Remember, the ultimate objective is to derive enjoyment from the game of golf. Positivity is a vital step in that direction. Let's embrace the challenge, stay positive, and enjoy the journey together!

### The Positivity Myth

Let's talk about the Positivity Myth and the misconceptions surrounding positive thinking. It's important to understand that positive thinking is not a magical solution that erases all problems and guarantees success. Many people mistakenly believe that being positive means ignoring or suppressing negative emotions, which is neither realistic nor helpful.

Positive thinking is not about avoiding difficulties or pretending they don't exist. It's about adopting a mindset that acknowledges challenges and looks for constructive ways to overcome them. It can be a powerful motivator, inspiring us to take action and pursue our goals. However, it's important to remember that positive thinking alone is not enough. It's like having a coupon for a discount—it's useful, but it doesn't guarantee success without putting in the necessary effort, resources, and resilience.

So, let's dispel the myth that positive thinking is a cure-all solution. It's a valuable tool, but it's only one part of the equation. Real success requires a combination of positive thinking, hard work, determination, and the ability to navigate challenges with resilience.

By understanding the true nature of positive thinking, we can develop a more balanced and realistic approach to our mindset. It's about embracing both the positive and negative aspects of life, learning from failures, and persisting in the face of obstacles. Remember, success comes from a combination of positivity, effort, and a willingness to adapt and grow.

### Negative Emotions CAN be Good too!

Sometimes, we might think that being positive means we should always be happy and never feel any negative emotions. But that's not true. Life is a mixture of good and not-so-good experiences, and it's okay to feel sad, angry, or frustrated sometimes. In fact, negative emotions are an important part of who we are and can help us grow as individuals.

In ancient societies, they understood the value of facing challenges and experiencing negative emotions. They believed it was essential for preparing young people to handle life's ups and downs. Nowadays, we live in a culture that often promotes constant optimism, which can make it seem like negative emotions are something to be avoided. But by acknowledging and understanding our negative emotions, we can learn more about ourselves and become emotionally stronger.

It's also important to remember that what we see on social media doesn't always reflect reality. People often share only the positive aspects of their lives, creating an image of constant happiness. But everyone faces challenges and struggles, even those who seem to be positive all the time.

Positivity doesn't mean we have to be happy all the time in every situation. Just like how our mood can change depending on different factors like the weather or other people's moods, it's natural for our emotions to fluctuate. Accepting these variations as part of being human is healthier and more realistic than trying to be positive all the time.

Having a healthy mindset means not only embracing positivity but also being willing to understand and confront our negative emotions. It's about finding a balance and navigating life's ups and downs with resilience and grace. It's important for teenagers and their parents to know that positivity is just one tool among many that can help us live fulfilling and balanced lives.

### Tricking Yourself Into Thinking Positively

Golf is not just about swinging clubs and hitting balls—it's also a game that challenges your mind. To succeed in golf, it's important to have a positive mindset. Here are some practical tips to help you cultivate positivity and improve your game.

### Focus on Your Target

Instead of worrying about hazards on the course, like bunkers or water bodies, focus on where you want the ball to go. Picture it landing on the fairway or the green. By directing your attention to the desired outcome, you're setting up a mental pathway for success.

### Visualize Success

Before each shot, close your eyes and imagine the perfect swing, the ball flying toward your target. This mental rehearsal helps prepare your mind for success and boosts your confidence.

### Watch Your Self-Talk

The way you talk to yourself matters. Keep your inner dialogue positive and empowering. Remind yourself of your skills and progress. Don't dwell on past mistakes—see each game as a fresh opportunity to learn and get better.

### Learn from Mistakes

When things don't go as planned, use it as a chance to reflect and learn. Think about what went wrong and how you can improve. Turn negative emotions into productive self-analysis.

### Be Kind to Yourself

Mistakes are part of learning and growing. Instead of being hard on yourself, treat mistakes as stepping stones on your journey to becoming better. Give yourself the encouragement and support you need.

### Remember the Big Picture

Each shot and each round of golf is part of a bigger journey. Keep your long-term goals in mind and appreciate the progress you're making. It's not just about one game—it's about the joy of the entire golfing experience.

### Know Why You Play

Remember why you love playing golf. Is it for the competition, the self-improvement, the camaraderie, or simply the joy of the game? Understanding your reasons will motivate you during tough times.

### Enjoy the Game

Golf is a game meant to be enjoyed. Embrace the triumphs, challenges, and setbacks. Every experience adds to your golfing journey. Appreciating the game will help you maintain a positive mindset.

By applying these strategies, you can cultivate a positive mindset that will improve your performance and make golf even more enjoyable. Remember, positivity is a powerful tool that can help you succeed on and off the course.

## Stories to Inspire: Tales of Triumph—Ally Mc-Donald's Conquest Over Negativity

Imagine you're playing an intense game of golf. You're focused and determined, but suddenly negative thoughts start creeping into your mind, making you doubt yourself. Don't worry, even the best athletes face this challenge. The story of Ally McDonald, a talented golfer, shows us how to conquer negativity and come out on top.

Ally, just like any other golfer, had to deal with negative thoughts. But what makes her special is how she turned those thoughts into a victory. During the 2020 LPGA Drive On Championship, Ally faced a tough moment at the 17th hole where she made a mistake. Most players would have let negativity take over, but not Ally.

She admitted that the mistake shook her up, but instead of giving in, she took control of her mind. She reminded herself to calm down and do what she had been doing in every round. She acknowledged the negative thoughts, but didn't let them ruin her game. Instead, she used them as motivation to regain her focus and went on to win the championship by a single stroke.

So, how did she do it? It's all about the ABCD of positivity:

A - Awareness: Ally recognized the negative thoughts.

B - Breathe: She took a deep breath to calm herself.

C - Calm: She stayed composed and focused.

D - Direct: She redirected her attention to the next shot.

Ally's story teaches us that negative thoughts don't have to bring us down. It's how we respond to them that matters. With a calm mind, a resilient spirit, and unwavering focus, we can turn challenges into victories.

Whether you're a teenager, a parent, or an aspiring athlete, remember Ally's story. It shows us that we have the power to overcome negativity and achieve our goals, no matter what obstacles we face. So, stay positive, stay focused, and keep pushing forward!

## Teeing Up: Actionable Steps to Improve Mental Toughness

### *For the Athlete*

1. *Understand the Positivity Myth:* Know that positive thinking is not about ignoring the negatives but rather is about reframing them into something constructive.

2. *Practice Neutral Thinking:* Learn to put a positive spin on negative thoughts rather than ignoring them. This shift in perspective can significantly impact your performance.

3. *Recognize the Power of Positivity:* Understand how a positive mindset can shape your performance on the golf course, ease anxiety, and even influence those around you.

4. *Visualize Success:* Use visualization techniques to

imagine your success on the golf course. Focus on what you want to achieve, not on what you fear might happen.

5. ***Channel Negative Emotion Productively:*** Instead of dwelling on negative emotions, use them to analyze and evaluate your performance. Remember the bigger picture, your larger goals, and why you're playing the game. Always keep in mind that golf is meant to be enjoyed.

# Your Journey
# Awaits...

Congratulations, young golfer! You've made it to the final chapter of this amazing book filled with wisdom and insights to transform not only your golf game but also your approach to life. It's time to wrap things up with a bang and leave you with a grand finale that will have you swinging for the stars!

Throughout this book, we've journeyed through the rough and smooth terrains of the golf course, discovering the secrets of success hidden in its emerald greens. From mastering the physical aspects of the game to unleashing the power of your mind, you've learned that golf is not just a sport but a captivating adventure of self-discovery.

So, what have we learned, young golfer? We've learned that perseverance is your caddy, resilience is your trusty club, and positivity is the magic ingredient that will elevate your game to new heights. We've learned that failure is not the end of the world, but a stepping stone to greatness. We've discovered that visualizing success and setting clear goals will guide your every swing, and that self-belief is the secret sauce that fuels your journey.

But here's the thing, my budding golf champion: the lessons you've learned on the fairway extend far beyond the boundaries of the golf course. Yes, you heard that right! Golf isn't just about hitting a little white ball into a hole—it's a metaphor for life itself. The skills you've honed here can be applied to any challenge you encounter in your journey through this wild and wonderful world.

Think about it. When you face a tough exam, a nerve-wracking audition, or even a friendship hiccup, what do you do? You approach it with the same determination and mental fortitude you bring to the golf course. You set your goals, visualize success, embrace failure as a learning opportunity, and maintain a positive mindset even when the odds seem stacked against you.

And guess what? By doing so, you become not only a better golfer but a better human being. You become a shining example of what it means to overcome obstacles, to chase your dreams with unwavering determination, and to embrace the joy of the journey itself. People will look at you in awe, not just for your swing, but for the way you navigate life's challenges with a twinkle in your eye and a spring in your step.

So, my young golf phenom, as you close this book and embark on your next golfing adventure, remember these lessons like your trusty caddies. Stay strong, stay focused, and never lose sight of the joy that golf—and life—brings. Keep swinging, keep learning, and above all, keep believing in yourself, because you, my friend, are destined for greatness.

And always remember: the fairway of life is waiting for you to step up and conquer it. With the skills you've acquired, the mindset you've cultivated, and the passion burning in your heart, there's no limit to what you can achieve. So, go out there, swing for the stars, and let your journey be filled with birdies, eagles, and the occasional hole-in-one.

May your golfing adventures be filled with laughter, ca-maraderie, and the sheer exhilaration of a well-played shot. And may the lessons you've learned on this incredible journey carry you to the pinnacle of success, not only in golf but in every aspect of your extraordinary life.

Now, young golfer, it's time to grab your clubs, step onto the fairway, and let the world witness your meteoric rise to greatness. The course is calling, and your destiny awaits. Swing high, swing true, and remember—life, like golf, is an adventure to be cherished and conquered!

# Chapter 10

# A Special Note of Thanks

D ear Reader,
  Thank you for joining us on this journey through the fairways, greens, and the greater game of life. By making it to the final page, you've shown the perseverance and commitment that "Swing for Success" is all about.

We hope that the lessons, strategies, and insights you found in this book will help you, or your young golfer, in mastering not just the mental game of golf, but also the challenges that life presents. Remember, golf is more than a game—it's a microcosm of the larger world, filled with victories, defeats, and opportunities for learning and growth.

We would be incredibly grateful if you could take a moment to leave an honest review on Amazon. Your feedback is vital—it helps us understand what we did well and what we can improve. More importantly, it helps other parents, coaches, and young athletes decide if this book might be beneficial for them.

Once again, thank you for picking up "Swing for Success: Mastering the Mental Game of Golf, Sports Psychology & Life Lessons for Kids". We sincerely hope that this book aids you on your journey towards becoming not just a better golfer, but a better person. Keep swinging for success, both on the course and off!

Best regards,

Phillip Chambers

Made in United States
Cleveland, OH
09 November 2024